FACILITATING TEACHER TEAMS AND AUTHENTIC PLCs

ASCD MEMBER BOOK

Many ASCD members received this book as
a member benefit upon its initial release.

Learn more at: www.ascd.org/memberbooks

FACILITATING TEACHER TEAMS AND AUTHENTIC PLCs

The Human Side of Leading People, Protocols, and Practices

DANIEL R. VENABLES

ASCD
ALEXANDRIA, VIRGINIA USA

1703 N. Beauregard St. • Alexandria, VA 22311-1714 USA
Phone: 800-933-2723 or 703-578-9600 • Fax: 703-575-5400
Website: www.ascd.org • E-mail: member@ascd.org
Author guidelines: www.ascd.org/write

Deborah S. Delisle, *Executive Director;* Stefani Roth, *Publisher;* Genny Ostertag, *Director, Content Acquisitions;* Julie Houtz, *Director, Book Editing & Production;* Miriam Calderone, *Editor;* Donald Ely, *Senior Graphic Designer;* Mike Kalyan, *Director, Production Services;* Circle Graphics, Inc., *Typesetter;* Kelly Marshall, *Senior Production Specialist*

PAPERBACK ISBN: 978-1-4166-2521-6   ASCD product #117004
PDF E-BOOK ISBN: 978-1-4166-2523-0; see Books in Print for other formats.

Quantity discounts are available: e-mail programteam@ascd.org or call 800-933-2723, ext. 5773, or 703-575-5773. For desk copies, go to www.ascd.org/deskcopy.

ASCD Member Book No. FY18-3. ASCD Member Books mail to Premium (P), Select (S), and Institutional Plus (I+) members on this schedule: Jan, PSI+; Feb, P; Apr, PSI+; May, P; Jul, PSI+; Aug, P; Sep, PSI+; Nov, PSI+; Dec, P. For current details on membership, see www.ascd.org/membership.

Library of Congress Cataloging-in-Publication Data

Names: Venables, Daniel R., author.
Title: Facilitating teacher teams and authentic PLCs : the human side of leading people, protocols, and practices / Daniel R. Venables.
Description: Alexandria, Virginia : ASCD, [2018] | Includes bibliographical references and index.
Identifiers: LCCN 2017040184 (print) | LCCN 2017049879 (ebook) | ISBN 9781416625230 (PDF) | ISBN 9781416625216 (pbk.)
Subjects: LCSH: Professional learning communities. | Teaching teams. | Educational leadership.
Classification: LCC LB1731 (ebook) | LCC LB1731 .V388 2017 (print) | DDC 371.14/8—dc23
LC record available at https://lccn.loc.gov/2017040184

27 26 26 25 24 23 22 21 20 19 18   1 2 3 4 5 6 7 8 9 10 11 12

for Ted Sizer (1932–2009)

FACILITATING TEACHER TEAMS AND AUTHENTIC PLCs

The Human Side of Leading People, Protocols, and Practices

ACKNOWLEDGMENTS

I dedicate this work to the late Ted Sizer, who has probably been the single biggest influence on my nearly 40-year career as an educator. He did more than inform me: he inspired me and deeply influenced my philosophy, attitudes, beliefs, and assumptions about teaching and learning. Moreover, thousands of educators could state the same claim. Ted questioned the status quo and took it head-on in many ways back when it was not terribly popular to do so. He did so because he cared about teachers and the kids in their charge. He was the Plato of education, raising questions and issues long before the rest of the (educational) population was ready to begin to discuss answers to the questions—let alone start asking them. Many of these issues are just now gaining traction in larger circles, often among educators who are too young to have heard of him.

Jude Pelchat also had a powerful role in helping me become a seasoned facilitator. I worked with Jude many years ago in my association with Sizer's Coalition of Essential Schools. As my mentor facilitator, she led by example. I can still hear her advice today during my most difficult and critical conversations with teachers. So thank you, Jude; I still listen.

I wish to thank my Grapple Institute cofacilitators, Cari Begin and Shawn Berry Clark, for working so hard with me to do the very best we can for the teachers we teach. Though I am hard on you at times, know that I have learned a lot from both of you.

I want to acknowledge the wonderful folks at ASCD who have given their all at every step in the process. Particularly, I am so very grateful to Genny Ostertag and Miriam Calderone. In addition to bringing their many ideas and suggestions to the work, they listened to my vision, really *got it,* and in turn did their best to incorporate it into this work.

Finally and, as always, I owe the greatest debt of thanks to my wife, Brady, who supported me and this work in both little and not-so-little ways during this book's winding and lengthy journey from idea to Amazon.

Daniel R. Venables
Lexington, South Carolina
July 2017

INTRODUCTION

Like my previous two books (*The Practice of Authentic PLCs* and *How Teachers Can Turn Data into Action*), this book was born of need. In my work helping dozens of schools and districts to implement authentic PLCs, I learned that it wasn't enough to educate teacher teams about what authentic PLCs are, what they do, and how they do it. That information was essential, to be sure, but without strong and knowledgeable leadership, these PLCs would have at best a marginal influence on student learning.

Accordingly, in early 2010, I started the Center for Authentic PLCs, through which I began offering professional development to schools and districts training teachers to be effective facilitators of PLCs. These trainings would eventually become the Grapple Institutes (see www.authenticplcs.com for more information).

Although nothing beats in-person training for learning about something as complex as facilitating PLCs, this book emerged as a kind of handbook for leading authentic PLCs, intended both for teachers who have been through the training and for those who have not. These pages address just about every topic related to facilitating PLCs that the Grapple Institutes cover.

It's Not About You

Facilitating teacher colleagues in doing the important work of authentic PLCs has been and continues to be one of the most challenging and rewarding endeavors I have pursued in my 30-plus years in education. For me, a major turning point in becoming a skilled facilitator was realizing that my effectiveness was directly dependent on my awareness of where my team members were—individually and collectively—in their understanding of and engagement with the work. In other words, my own understanding and readiness to embrace a new idea or protocol matter less than *their* level of understanding and readiness. I realized that for PLCs to rise to the next level, facilitators need to be in tune with where their teachers are and contribute just the right thing to move them forward.

Good instructors in any field—yoga, piano, football, you name it—take their students to the next level; *great* instructors take their students to the next level *without skipping any.* To be able to do so, they must be continually aware of students' present understanding as well as their readiness for the next thing. Such is also true of PLC facilitators.

Developing this finely tuned awareness and acting on it accordingly may seem to be a daunting task, but with the aid of this book and some practice, it will become second nature. In the meantime, ask yourself, "What do my team members need *right now* to move forward in their knowledge, understanding, and readiness?" It's not terribly different from what master teachers ask themselves during classroom instruction.

What's in This Book

Facilitating Teacher Teams and Authentic PLCs is divided into two parts: "Facilitating Teachers and Teacher Teams" and "Facilitating Tasks of Authentic PLCs." In Part 1, I discuss the human side of facilitating PLCs—that is, facilitating the people in them—and provide the skill set necessary to do it effectively. In Part 2, I offer targeted guidance in facilitating specific protocols and activities typically used in PLC work. Because each protocol has its own nuances and potential pitfalls, I designed Part 2 as a "preemptive strike" to help facilitators anticipate and address the obstacles and jams that commonly pop up during use of the protocols. Part 2 also provides tips for making each protocol the richest possible experience for the teacher team. To enhance facilitation, many of the tools and protocols described throughout this book appear in full in the Appendix. In addition, you can access some of these resources at http://www.ascd.org/ASCD/pdf/books/Venables2017forms.pdf.

There are many ideas in this book that require no direct action; they are there to inform the reader and raise awareness of the salient aspects of navigating the interpersonal waters of leading a team of teachers. In other cases, reading is informative but insufficient; some things need to be practiced with teachers in a real live PLC. There is a third type of information in the book that may not require direct practice but can best be understood and internalized through discussion with other teacher leaders. As you will see in Chapter 3, I refer to this practice as *constructing community knowledge*.

The Vignettes

Throughout this book, you will find short vignettes that offer additional clarity and insight into the nuances of facilitation. Each "Fly on the Wall" section includes a narrative describing a scene from a fictional PLC's meeting, with footnotes providing brief analyses of particular points of interest. I suggest that when you are reading the text with colleagues (for example, in a book study), you first read the scene without looking at the footnotes. Then discuss why you think various parts of the vignette have been highlighted for analysis. After this discussion, read the footnotes and see where your thinking and understanding align with my own.

Venablisms

First of all, this is not my term; that would be really haughty. This appellation was coined by several participants at a Grapple Institute who observed that I uttered certain truisms over and over again in an effort to highlight any area where they applied. A broken record, me. The Grapple participants compiled a list and called them "Venablisms." I include them in this book not because I was flattered (although I was), but because they are *that* important. Each of these tenets is of paramount importance and gets at the heart of leading teams. (The only one the Grapple participants missed—no doubt because I say it in jest—happens to apply to the rest of the list: *Bumper stickers and T-shirts should be issued.*)

A Note on Terms and Titles

Although the terms *PLC* and *teacher team* are not synonymous—it is possible for a school to have teacher teams that would not, by my definition, constitute PLCs—I nonetheless use the words interchangeably for simplicity and clarity. In a similar way, I use the titles *leader, facilitator,* and *coach* interchangeably to refer to those who lead PLCs in their schools.

There Is Learning in the Balance

Lest we forget, as we spend untold hours working with adults, that it is the students who are the primary benefactors of our labor, here's a reminder: this work is about kids. Teachers in a PLC have the right and responsibility to throw the *What does this have to do with student learning?* flag whenever our discussions veer off track.

Indeed, in all of our work together, we must constantly remind ourselves and one another that ***there is learning in the balance.*** The quality of the decisions we make and the swiftness with which we make them greatly affect the education of our students. Time is ticking away for *these* students in *our* charge *this* year as we wait for 100 percent buy-in, or postpone a sensible initiative until next year, or avoid having hard conversations with an ineffective teacher, or make choices that are convenient for us rather than right for the learning of our children.

This truth provides the beacon that lights our way as we make our decisions and prioritize our focus, and it provides the strength we need when we're having the hard conversations with one another. When we truly put students at the forefront, difficult decisions become surprisingly easy to make.

VENABLISMS: NON-SLOGANS OF FACILITATING AUTHENTIC PLCS*

The epithet "Venablisms" was coined by a group of teachers attending my Grapple Institute to refer to certain things I say repeatedly throughout the three-day training. Collectively, the "non-slogans" that follow form the heart of authentic facilitation.

- Trust the process.
- This is about kids.
- Build the team before you need it.
- There is learning in the balance.
- Brave the skinny branches.
- Separate the work from the person.
- Facilitators share last.
- Do ask, don't tell.
- Candor with care.
- Challenges precede growth.
- It's not about where you are.
- Trust your instincts.
- At the heart of it, PLCs are a human endeavor.
- Substance with safety.
- Debrief. Debrief. Debrief.
- Do what you say you're going to do.
- Lead the team for the team.
- Strengthen the team at every opportunity.
- Make the meeting meaningful.
- Elevate, don't evaluate (the work).

* Each Venablism represents a core edict in facilitating authentic PLCs developed by Daniel R. Venables. Each is printed in boldface and italics wherever it appears in the text of this book, and each is the subject of a short video in a series titled *From the Human Side (of Facilitating PLCs)*. These videos will periodically be posted to www.authenticplcs.com/thehumanside.

Part 1:
The Human Side of Facilitating Teachers and Teacher Teams

When it comes down to it, facilitating our fellow teachers is an essentially human endeavor. In most cases, teachers who have been asked (or who have volunteered) to facilitate their teacher teams are colleagues, not administrators. Because they occupy the same position on the totem pole as the rest of the teachers in the PLC and have no special supervisory powers, their effectiveness as facilitators depends significantly on their relationships with their fellow team members. In fact, their leadership in the team is based on these relationships; they have no leverage other than this. Thus, the health of these relationships is paramount. Part 1 of this book accordingly addresses the essentials of facilitating colleagues, building trust and buy-in, and dealing with interpersonal obstacles.

1 | FACILITATION ESSENTIALS

Human and Social Capital

Schools used to pour all of their professional development dollars into building their *human capital*—that is, improving the quality, knowledge, and skill sets of individual teachers. The rationale was that teachers who attended conferences or participated in other professional development opportunities would return to their schools brimming with knowledge and pass their learning on to their colleagues. In many cases, however, this simply didn't happen, so the funds invested in sending a single teacher to a conference yielded relatively small returns—which led to little improvement in classroom instruction on any scale.

Today, thanks in large part to the research of Dr. Carrie Leana of the University of Pittsburgh and others, we are learning that building *social capital* is a more effective professional development strategy. In contrast to human capital, social capital refers to the quality of the interactions among teachers in a department or school. Schools with high social capital show significantly higher gains in student learning than do schools with low social capital—even when those schools have moderately low human capital. Leana writes,

> When the relationships among teachers in a school are characterized by high trust and frequent interaction—that is, when social capital is strong—student achievement scores improve. . . . We also found that even low-ability teachers can perform as well as teachers of average ability *if* they have strong social capital. Strong social capital can go a long way toward offsetting any disadvantages students face when their teachers have low human capital. (2011, pp. 33, 34)

This is not to say that schools should never bother improving their human capital; incorporating both forms of teacher professional development is ideal (Figure 1.1 offers examples of actions that promote both types of capital). If schools want to get the most bang for their professional development buck, however, they should invest heavily in developing the social capital of their teachers and teacher teams. A great

FIGURE 1.1 | Actions That Boost Social and Human Capital

Actions That Boost Social Capital	Actions That Boost Human Capital
• Learning together by reading articles, watching videos, and discussing findings • Training PLC facilitators to understand and deal with interpersonal team dynamics • Holding teams responsible for setting their own goals • Holding teams responsible for identifying and solving their own problems • Building PLC meeting time into the daily schedule • Instituting regular, consistent peer observations • Reflecting on goals and progress toward goals on a regular basis and celebrating successes • Fostering team dependence • Planning instruction together	• Sending individual teachers to professional conferences • Inviting a speaker or trainer to address the faculty • Setting individualized professional goals • Depending on individual teacher action plans to support low-performing teachers • Setting up mentor teacher programs • Conducting administrative classroom observations • Holding one-on-one teacher-administrator conferences • Fostering principal dependence • Having instructional coaches

way to spike the social capital of a school is to focus priority on the school's PLCs. If the quality of teacher interactions in a school's PLCs improves, there is likely to be a commensurate gain in student learning.

Why Are PLC Facilitators Indispensable?

Although PLCs are an effective way to build social capital, not all PLCs are created equal. More specifically, ensuring effective *facilitation* of PLCs is key; simply assembling teams and sending them on their way is inadequate. As someone who works with schools throughout the United States developing authentic PLCs and training facilitators, I firmly believe that every PLC should have a person designated as the facilitator.

There are PLC models available that don't call for a facilitator. The thinking behind such models is that "we're all in this together," and their structure is based on a model of shared leadership. In theory, a teacher team that is able to facilitate itself sounds great, but I have rarely seen this model work in practice. Usually, shared leadership in this context means no leadership at all. Discussions veer off track, time is wasted, and the focus shifts from teaching and learning to matters only tangentially, if at all, related to student learning. As a result, the growth of such a team is very slow, and anything meaningful the team achieves could have been accomplished by a facilitator-led PLC in half the time. Slow progress and a lack of focus aren't the only drawbacks of this model; more serious is what happens when interpersonal conflicts or other obstacles arise and there's no well-trained facilitator to guide the group to a resolution.

The Role of the Facilitator

A PLC facilitator's primary role is to increase and maintain the social capital in his or her teacher team. If team members are engaging in quality interactions focused on teaching and learning, then their students' achievement will improve. This job comes with many other responsibilities, including

- Guiding the team through the steps of protocols.
- Asking thought-provoking questions that challenge conventional thinking and push the discussion to a deeper level.
- Promoting and modeling honesty and respect in discussions.
- Ensuring that all voices are heard.
- Maintaining team members' emotional safety during discussions.
- Keeping the team focused and moving it forward when it's stuck.
- Mediating disagreements and helping the team navigate the sometimes-turbulent waters of interpersonal dynamics.
- Being able to step back, particularly when being emotionally drawn into a problematic group dynamic.
- Working for the good of the team.

The last bullet point touches on one of the most important responsibilities of a PLC facilitator. In 1985, when dozens of the biggest names in music came together to record the charity single "We Are the World," a sign posted outside the studio admonished the artists to "Please check your egos at the door." This sign served to remind participants that the goal of the project was to help others—not to boost egos or careers. Similarly, the Code of Ethics I share in *The Practice of Authentic PLCs* includes the credo "Leave your ego at the door, but bring your brains inside" (Venables, 2011, p. 146) to remind PLC facilitators and members alike to put aside self-interest and call their brains to the fore so that they can think deeply about the important work at hand. Our decisions, actions, and priorities must not be tainted by what serves our own egos but instead be guided by what is best for student learning.

Most of the PLC facilitator's responsibilities just listed will fall into place as long as he or she strives to keep the team's interactions at a high level. The remainder of this chapter explores what I refer to as facilitation essentials: balancing content and process, figuring out appropriate facilitation styles for different tasks, building an effective team before you need one, empowering the team, honing nonverbal communication skills, and using protocols.

Balancing Content and Process

One of the biggest challenges PLC facilitators face is balancing *content* and *process*. To illustrate, guiding a PLC through the steps of a protocol requires the facilitator to move team members through each segment, announcing what is supposed to happen and why and refereeing the discussion as team members make contributions. The facilitator may also make contributions to the discussion, as she is a full-fledged member of the PLC and, like any member of the team, may have valuable insights related to the topic. These are all concerns of *content*.

At the same time, the PLC facilitator must observe how the protocol is going, asking herself questions like *Are all members contributing? Is the discussion superficial or shallow? Is the body language of any member communicating discomfort with what is being said? Is the conversation straying off topic? Is any member dominating air time? Is the current segment of the protocol running over time? If so, should I allow the conversation to continue or move on to the next piece? Is the discussion helping teacher X, who has put his work on the table for all to review?* These are all concerns of *process*.

Whereas all other team members can fully immerse themselves in the content of the PLC's work, the facilitator must necessarily concern herself with both content *and* process if she is to keep things moving smoothly, maximize the benefits of the discussion at hand, and maintain high-quality discourse. This dual responsibility of maintaining the social capital of her team while engaging as an active member herself can be exhausting—but it's crucial, ensuring that her team will get the most out of the experience and that student learning will improve as a result of the team's work. And isn't that why facilitators are there in the first place?

Figuring Out the Right Facilitation Style

As facilitators, we bring to the table our unique personalities, just as we do as classroom teachers. Early in my career, I was told by an administrator that 90 percent of good teaching boils down to personality. I'm not sure that I would place the percentage quite so high, but I absolutely concur with the sentiment of her claim and suspect a similar conjecture could be made about PLC facilitators.

Some PLC coaches are soft-spoken and emit a warm, caring persona; others who are more "Type A" feel driven to get things done and check items off the meeting's agenda; still others are no-nonsense but exhibit a permeating sense of humor as they lead the team through various tasks. All of these styles, and many others, can make for effective facilitation. But facilitators must also bear in mind that, independent of their particular style, there are some PLC tasks or protocols that require stronger (or tighter) facilitation and others that call for softer (or looser) facilitation. The decision to facilitate in a tight or loose way should be dictated more by the task at hand than by a facilitator's preferences or style.

For example, a PLC coach would do well to loosely facilitate a discussion about updating the team's existing set of norms but tightly facilitate a text-based discussion. If he is too loose in his facilitation of the latter task, the conversation will quickly veer off course and may turn into autobiographical recitations from one or two particularly vocal team members. When this happens, it is immensely difficult to draw the PLC back to the text.

Many considerations go into a facilitator's decision of how loosely or tightly to run particular parts of a meeting. Factors such as PLC members' level of trust and buy-in, the facilitator's level of experience, the type of task at hand, and how seasoned the team is all contribute to the coach's choice of facilitation style. As such, there is no carved-in-stone list of which PLC tasks call for loose facilitation and which call for tight facilitation, although I do discuss facilitation pointers for various protocols in Part 2 of this book. For now, suffice it to say that PLC coaches—especially new ones—should err on the side of too tight rather than too loose. Like teachers who run an extra-tight ship at the beginning of the school year, they can always back off a bit and loosen their facilitation in time.

Building a Team Before You Need It

I am regularly asked by schools and school districts to do one of the following: (1) build authentic PLCs from the ground up or (2) retool existing PLCs that have floundered in their work, failed to improve student achievement, or morphed into little more than planning or teacher gripe sessions. Personally, I would always rather create a school's PLCs from scratch than save the established but ineffective ones. Unluckily for me, more schools are in the second camp than in the first.

My first step in improving a school's ineffective PLCs is to find out the reasons for their lack of success. I discuss some of these reasons in detail in Chapter 2, but here

I will focus on the most common reason for a PLC's failure: the team has neglected to build a foundation of collaboration among its members. Often, the members of such a team have plunged into the work and begun to set agendas and norms, examine data, and look at teacher work right away without taking time to establish themselves as a strong team. This well-intentioned but misguided way of working usually stems from an ill-trained facilitator who did not realize the importance of engaging the team in experiences that lay a strong initial foundation of collaboration and trust. As a result, the norms set by the team were likely dictated by a few vocal members, and teacher work brought to the table was probably cursorily reviewed and mostly *celebrated*—no matter how good or bad it was—because the teachers in the PLC didn't know how to pose questions about or challenge a colleague's work. Worse yet, the team may have brought up questions or dilemmas in too harsh a way, or the feedback may have been received too defensively, leaving all members with a bad taste in their mouths and feeling ill disposed toward presenting their work again—or engaging in any protocols at all.

The damage done in such a scenario is significant—all because the PLC was more an ill-led collection of individuals than it was a well-facilitated *team* ready to collaborate. In Chapter 2, I delve more deeply into matters of trust and buy-in. For now, the crux is that at some point in the life of an authentic PLC, there *will* be hard issues, delicate subjects, and discussions that require participants to take risks, be vulnerable, and trust their fellow PLC members. When they get there, they had better be a strong, established team ready to tackle the challenge. ***Build the team before you need it.***

Empowering the Team

High-functioning PLCs exude a clear sense of empowerment in their work. To an outside observer, the members of a successful PLC are all deeply engaged in and committed to the work at hand. All members contribute to the discussion knowing that their remarks matter and that they will be received as valid contributions by their teammates. Team members tacitly embrace personal responsibility for the outcome of their collective labor; they all appear to own every piece of what is happening during the meeting.

The observer of such a team may not be able to tell who the facilitator is; there is no dominant voice or other immediate sign of who is "in charge." The identity of the facilitator eventually becomes clear because of the profusion of questions she continually asks of both the team as a whole and individual members. These questions are thoughtful and thought-provoking; they have no evaluative or judgmental component, nor are they thinly disguised suggestions. She asks PLC members to push or challenge their thinking, clarify comments, gain more information. The team responds well to these questions, and ideas spring forth at a dizzying pace. The seriousness of what the PLC members are doing is palpable: humor is injected freely, but it never throws the team off task. The outside observer would be impressed by the professionalism of the group and get the distinct impression that everyone sitting at the meeting wants to be there. The synergy of this team's interactions is a clear indication that the PLC is greater than the sum of its parts.

All these characteristics of a high-functioning PLC serve as evidence that the team members feel empowered—and, more to the point, that the facilitator of this PLC has empowered the team. She has given team members a voice and validated that voice. She carefully guides the discourse without evaluation or admonishment. She shows all individuals the same abundant respect that they afford her. There is a sense that the facilitator will follow up on suggestions made by the team. Occasionally, the burst of ideas subsides, and there are stretches of silence. These don't feel awkward; they indicate neither that the team has exhausted all thinking on the topic nor that the members are no longer engaged. Quite the opposite: the silence is a snapshot of what reflective thinking can look like. The PLC facilitator has modeled her own comfort with silence and, in this way, has engendered a tacit norm that silence is OK—that thinking at a deep level requires it. Although this may seem to be a trivial attribute, I can generally tell how seasoned a PLC facilitator is from his or her level of comfort with silence during team discussions.

This high-functioning PLC didn't just get lucky; the facilitator deliberately took a few key steps to empower her team. The following sections explore these steps.

Believing in Team Members

Empowering a teacher team means empowering each teacher on the team. In all cases, it requires an assumption on the part of the facilitator that each teacher, regardless of where he or she is on the buy-in/buy-out continuum (see Chapter 2), is able and willing to engage in high-quality collaboration with his or her colleagues. When a facilitator truly believes that team members *can*—and clearly communicates this belief through his or her engagement with the team members—they most often *will*. Inversely, if the facilitator doubts team members' ability and willingness—and communicates that message—then the team will very often prove him or her right. This simple principle of believing in teachers and demonstrating that belief in all interactions with them works amazingly well. People in all professions generally achieve not to the highest level of *expectation* placed upon them, but to the highest level of *belief* by leaders that they can (Covey, 2014).

Giving Voice and Choice—and Following Up

Giving the teacher team voice and choice in every possible decision facing the PLC is a good way to empower the team—but it will only work if it's not an empty gesture. It is imperative that the facilitator follow up by listening to team members' voices and honoring their choices. In my own role as facilitator, the decisions I need to make unilaterally are few and far between. Most of the time, the team can decide with me—and then I have the responsibility to go with what they have chosen, even in cases where I would have gone in a different direction. The only exception is when team members' choice is not driven by what is best for students but made for less-honorable reasons (e.g., it's the easiest, most comfortable, or lowest-risk option). If this is not the case, and the team makes its choice in earnest for the right reasons, the facilitator has the responsibility to follow up with the team's decision. Few things endear PLC members to the facilitator more than when the facilitator follows up on the team's decisions and does what she promised to do.

Delegating Tasks

One of the most common pitfalls inexperienced facilitators encounter is trying to do everything themselves. No matter how well-intentioned this might be, it is harmful for two reasons. First, it detracts from the facilitator's primary role—increasing and maintaining the team's social capital—and its attendant responsibilities. The facilitator must maintain a strong focus on leading the team through the task at hand and delegate other roles (e.g., timekeeping, recording meeting notes, bringing X or Y to the next meeting) to the other teachers on the team. Facilitators should get in the habit of asking for volunteers to do these tasks and, if none comes forward, directly requesting the help of a teammate: "Carla, would you bring copies of our curriculum map for Unit 4 to the next meeting so we can take a look at it?" or "Jimmy, would you mind being timekeeper for this protocol?" My routine line is "OK, we all decided last meeting that we would do X; who would like to do Y, Z, and W?" Simple, direct, and effective.

The second danger in not delegating tasks is that if the facilitator does everything, the team will *always* expect him or her to do everything. This leads to a lack of investment from team members. Effective PLC facilitators get teachers on the team to put some skin in the game. Teachers who invest their time and effort for the good of the team, even in small or relatively insignificant ways, are more likely to feel as though they are a part of the whole and invest themselves in pursuing the team's common goals. Multiply this effect by six or seven teachers, and the team as a whole becomes considerably empowered.

Honing Nonverbal Communication Skills

When I am asked to be part of a conference call with the administrators of a school or district, I often suggest that we converse in a Google hangout. Google hangouts are video conferences, much like Skype, that permit as many as 10 participants and include a screen-sharing capability that lets users share documents, graphics, or statistics as well as see one another's faces. Facial expressions and other physical cues are powerful signs of how people are thinking and feeling.

Classroom teachers get very good at reading their students' facial expressions and body language. This skill becomes useful in facilitating a team of teachers during a PLC meeting. Picking up nonverbal cues that indicate confusion, disagreement, trepidation, reflective thinking, boredom, off-topic thinking, hesitancy to speak or ask a question, irritation with another member, skepticism with what is being shared, and so forth can provide valuable information to the facilitator. Becoming adept at observing these nonverbal cues and addressing the thoughts and feelings they indicate not only show PLC members that the facilitator is paying attention and cares about the members of the team but also can defuse a situation that might blow up into a bigger issue if verbalized. It's important not to get hyper-focused on our agendas or the steps of a protocol lest we miss what is happening right in front of us in the minds and hearts of our teammates.

Using Protocols

The use of protocols has become widespread in teacher teams and PLCs throughout the United States—and for good reason. If you're unfamiliar with protocols, here's my definition:

> A protocol is a set of guidelines for having a focused, structured conversation about some aspect of teaching and learning. Teacher teams use them for a wide range of applications. There are protocols for looking at student work, looking at teacher work, having discussions centered on an article or piece of text, reviewing student data, analyzing a dilemma a teacher might be having, and many other purposes. (Venables, 2015a, para. 4)

Protocols are useful tools for teacher teams, particularly for facilitators. The structure that protocols provide helps the facilitator keep discussions focused, fair, and substantive. Protocols that are used to discuss teacher work (e.g., a teacher-designed assessment, a lesson plan, a teaching strategy or activity, or a teacher-made rubric) culminate in practical suggestions for making specific improvements to the work under discussion. As a rule, after a PLC goes through a protocol, the team members follow up by applying their learning in the classroom.

Throughout this book, I incorporate vignettes illustrating the work and interactions of a fictional 8th grade social studies PLC. These "Fly on the Wall" scenarios are intended to illuminate, extend, and bring together the ideas discussed in the chapter. Here is a look at the PLC's interpersonal context:

- **Angie** is the hard-working, selfless facilitator of the team. She is in her eighth year of teaching middle school social studies and has a reputation as a good teacher. She has been trained to facilitate and is eager to put her newly acquired skill set into practice.
- **Bruce**, the assistant football coach of the school district's high school, has been teaching for 15 years. He is skeptical about PLC work and generally uninterested in what is happening until the discussion bears consequence that will affect his 8th grade son, who is in Cassandra's class. Bruce's lack of interest is hardly clandestine; he has been known to write football plays during meetings. His teacher ego is solid, even if his teaching at times is not.
- **Cassandra** has spent her entire 10-year career teaching at the same middle school. She is a very good teacher, adored by kids and parents alike. Her personality is dominant, practical, and opinionated. Cassandra has bought into the PLC work because she can see the difference it can make for kids. Her teacher identity is as strong as her opinions tend to be.
- **Devin** is a quiet, sincere, sometimes wryly funny teacher who is in his fifth year of teaching. He doesn't make waves, but he has no spark, either. His teaching ability is average. Although he is not *committed* to the work of the PLC, he is *compliant* and does what is asked of him. His contributions to the PLC discussions are few and tend to be superficial.
- **Evelyn**, like Cassandra, is opinionated, but she also has a very nurturing side. She has been teaching for 28 years and is formerly the lead teacher on the team. She is National Board Certified, but an observer of her class wouldn't necessarily see anything stellar going on; she is very traditional and tends to spoon-feed students. Still, she is well liked by the community.

The following Fly on the Wall explores our 8th grade PLC's first day using a protocol.

FLY ON THE WALL

The Scene:
The First Day of Protocols
(Part 1)*

What Happened

After engaging her team in a brief discussion about what protocols are, why they are useful, and how they differ from activities, Angie outlines the key steps of the Notice & Wonder Protocol for Data [see Chapter 8], passes out copies of the protocol, and asks her team to read it quietly.[1]

Angie begins the Notice & Wonder Protocol for Data with her team, reading each step immediately before executing it. She emphasizes the difference between *Notice* and *Wonder* statements so that the team is clear.[2] Even so, Evelyn has a clarifying question, which Angie answers.

After Angie recruits a timekeeper (Bruce) and a scribe for the Notice and Wonder statements (Evelyn), the team proceeds with the Notice round. There is no discussion, except as in the following exchange:

Evelyn: I notice the girls scored 14 percentage points higher than the boys on figurative language.

Devin: Maybe they talk more?

Angie: Let's try and remember that our goal is just to observe things in the data. Please don't speculate on possible causes.[3]

The team moves to the Wonder round. Angie reminds the teachers of the characteristics of Wonder statements and tells them that she may ask follow-up questions during this round. After a half-dozen Wonder statements, the following exchange occurs:

Cassandra: I wonder if on Standard SS8H3, they really understand the causes of the American Revolution or are simply memorizing the causes.

Angie: Let's explore that a moment. [To the team] What are we doing or not doing that might be encouraging memorizing versus understanding the causes?[4]

For the next eight minutes, the team engages in a short but substantive discussion that has clear connections to instruction.[5]

---

*See also The First Day of Protocols (Part 2) on page 69.

(continued)

What's Worth Noting

[1]Before the team even begins the protocol, Angie has explained its purpose, provided a general outline of what to expect during the protocol, and given team members time to read it in advance of doing it. This encourages a degree of comfort and open-mindedness among team members as they embark on something new.

[2]Protocols run smoothly when the members of a PLC are crystal-clear on what they are expected to do in each segment of the protocol. By taking the time to read through each step and preemptively clear up any possible confusion between two related ideas (in this case, Notice versus Wonder statements), Angie lays out a smooth path for her team to follow.

[3]Devin's remark, although thoughtless and verging on sexist, was meant to be humorous and probably stemmed from his own nervousness. However, Angie called out his break from the protocol as though he were seriously posing an observation. To be sure, it is important for her to call out members when they are not following the protocol or when they say something offensive to others. In this case, however, she misread Devin's intent and came off as somewhat militant in following the "rules." Admonishing a teacher for a passing joke can actually take the team farther off track than simply moving on, so facilitators should carefully consider their interventions.

[4]It is imperative that, at every possible turn, the PLC conversation get to instruction. This is where the seeds of instructional improvement are often planted. When Cassandra made her Wonder statement, Angie seized the moment to dive more deeply into matters of instruction. Seasoned PLC facilitators are continually looking for member-initiated opportunities to discuss instruction.

[5]In time, with a little persistence on Angie's part, making connections to and discussing instruction become the culture of the PLC. When this happens, members of the PLC initiate the instructional connections with little prodding from the facilitator.

In Part 2 of this book, I discuss specific protocols and strategies to facilitate them and maximize the gains they yield. Before we get there, however, we must focus on developing strong, authentic PLCs. To that end, Chapter 2 examines the nature of teacher trust and buy-in—and how to get it.

2 | BUILDING TRUST AND BUY-IN

Professional learning communities are about as ubiquitous in education these days as Chromebook laptops and interactive whiteboards. Most schools have some form of teacher teams that foster collaboration and team planning. But the good ones—the ones I refer to as authentic PLCs—engage in pursuits more serious than simple collaborative planning. Members of these PLCs look critically at student and teacher work, offer constructive feedback to one another, design quality common assessments, review and respond to all sorts of student data, and respond with action when students aren't learning. These are the high-functioning PLCs, the ones whose members embrace differences in opinion, are willing to ask the hard questions of one another, and have built a level of trust and candor more common in family units than in groups of teachers with common planning time. These PLCs are interdependent systems, and their individual members credit the team for their successes. Teachers in these teams make quick progress in honing their craft and improve themselves continually.

The bedrock of all high-functioning PLCs is trust. But trust doesn't happen just because teachers of a given subject or grade level are granted a common planning period. In this chapter, we'll look closely at both impediments and contributors to trust and its close kin, buy-in.

The Nature of Buy-In

As an education consultant who spends most days working with schools, administrators, and teachers to implement and lead authentic PLCs, I get asked a lot of questions. The most frequently asked one is "How do we get teachers to buy in to this?" I respond that there is no one way to ensure teacher buy-in when implementing any change, but there are many ways—some small and others not so small—to maximize teacher buy-in.

What exactly *is* buy-in? Buying in to what? Buy-in is an amorphous, intangible commodity that is characterized by a willingness to embrace and try in earnest some new idea or way of doing things. By this definition, it challenges the status quo—the usual way of doing things—and, in turn, challenges teachers to think anew, break old paradigms, be willing to take risks, and be willing to fail (at least at first or in little ways). By its very nature, buy-in requires trust, particularly in those at the helm of the new change. It requires teachers to let go of old habits and ways of doing things and replace them with new and better ways of operating. In many cases, buy-in does not require teachers to change *what* they are doing but to rethink *how* they are doing it. For example, the Common Core Standards for Mathematical Content (National Governors Association Center for Best Practices [NGA Center] & Chief Council of State School Officers [CCSSO], 2010) (the what) are not terribly new or earth-shattering: they include content that is essentially the same as that published in the NCTM's *Curriculum and Evaluation Standards for School Mathematics* that came out in 1989. The real change, and the greatest challenge to most math teachers, comes in implementing the Common Core Standards for Mathematical Practice (the how). This set of standards is much more radical than the content standards themselves are.

Asking teachers to buy in to a new policy or process, such as a new system for entering semester grades, may require them to do things differently and thus be met with some resistance. After the initial grumblings, however, most teachers adapt and habituate to this kind of new procedure. By contrast, asking teachers to buy in to implementation of authentic PLCs (or retooling of existing ineffective PLCs) requires them to embrace a change in school *culture*. The change is less about what they do than about who they are and what they value. Buying in to a new culture is slower, more complex, and more challenging for teachers to do than buying in to a new procedure or policy. For this reason, what may work in changing the way a faculty carries out a procedure often fails in attempting to change faculty culture. In all my travels, I have never once witnessed authentic PLCs becoming part of a faculty's culture because the principal issued an administrative mandate. Although principals may have had a heavy hand in introducing PLCs to the school campus and creating the environment and skills necessary for authentic PLCs to flourish, they can only shape and guide faculty culture—they can't mandate it to be a certain way. ***At its heart, this work is a human endeavor.***

Figure 2.1 lists a variety of factors that contribute to teacher buy-in as well as to its opposite—what I call teacher "buy-out."

The Continuum of Teacher Buy-In

Teacher buy-in is not a binary phenomenon; generally speaking, teachers don't either buy in to PLCs or reject them. Instead, they land somewhere on a continuum of teacher buy-in. Although some teachers reside firmly at the pole of buy-in or the pole of buy-out, most teachers are not so polarized in their position and typically lean

FIGURE 2.1 | Factors Contributing to Teacher Buy-In and Buy-Out

Factors Contributing to Teacher Buy-In in PLCs	Factors Contributing to Teacher Buy-Out in PLCs
• Teachers feel integrated into the group. • Teachers don't feel that their time is being wasted. • Teachers are getting something accomplished. • Facilitators are transparent at all times. • Teachers are offered choice and invited to offer input. • Meetings have purpose and yield outcomes. • PLCs get results. • Work is focused on teacher needs. • Time is allotted in the master schedule for PLC work. • Team members feel empowered. • Students are the main focus. • Meetings are meaningful, focused on identifying and solving problems. • PLC work relates to teachers' immediate implementation in the classroom. • Teacher concerns are validated during meetings. • Meetings are organized and well planned. • Teams accomplish things at meetings. • The powers above have buy-in. • All team members feel that the work is valuable to them personally.	• PLCs generate additional unnecessary work. • The facilitator is not prepared. • Meetings waste teachers' time and don't apply to their work. • Teachers feel that the directive to form PLCs may result in additional work that overwhelms them. • Meetings are consistently off task (e.g., side conversations are common). • Tasks or requested changes are assigned at the last minute and teachers aren't given an appropriate timeline to accomplish them. • Teachers feel insecure about the quality of their work. • Facilitators lead with know-it-all attitudes. • Meetings waste time and accomplish nothing. • Expectations across PLCs are inconsistent. • Teachers feel afraid to make mistakes. • The paradigm shift from an old way of teaching to more innovative approaches is met with resistance from some quarters, which then spreads to the rest of the team. • The powers above dictate rather than collaborate. • Ideas are abandoned before they're seen through. • Conflicts aren't resolved.

Every item on this list was generated by the participants of a Grapple One Institute held in West Palm Beach, Florida, on September 8, 2016.

either in the direction of buying in or in the direction of buying out. The distribution is not a bell curve; few teachers are smack-dab in the middle. Figure 2.2 gives a rundown of what the different points on the continuum look like.

Teachers' positions along this continuum tend to change with time. When good things are happening in the PLC, teachers' positions shift toward the buy-in pole of the continuum. This direction of movement is more common than the opposite, but if a PLC is ineffective or unproductive, teachers who initially bought in may begin to question their choice and move in the direction of buy-out. One of the most important things PLC facilitators should keep in mind is that there is a danger in labeling teachers based on where they are *today*. Given that teachers' positions on the continuum are likely to change, facilitators should note where their team members are today, knowing that they may not be there tomorrow, and work with them where they are. Labeling team members brands them in a way that can freeze their position on the continuum and make it more difficult for facilitators to help move them forward.

100 Percent Buy-In?

Another question I am often asked is "How do we get everyone on the faculty to buy in to this?"

There is a prevailing misconception that any reform effort or endeavor that asks teachers to change their thinking and behavior requires 100 percent buy-in to succeed. Not only is 100 percent buy-in nearly impossible to achieve—at least in the early stages of change—but expending vast amounts of energy trying to achieve this unrealistic percentage also causes many noble efforts to burn out before they even ignite. Getting 100 percent buy-in from the faculty is *not* the goal. The goal is to have high-functioning, authentic PLCs working collaboratively in a way that maximizes student learning and transforms the school's culture. We cannot wait until every teacher fully embraces any new idea or way of doing things. If we did, nothing would ever change. And while we wait, ***there is learning in the balance.*** Many successful reform efforts have been launched by a minority of faculty members. Although having high buy-in numbers helps, what matters more is *who* is buying in and what their relationship is with other faculty. We all know those teachers who are natural leaders among their colleagues, whether or not they have an official leadership title within the school community. These teachers have "street cred" and a great deal of influence over their peers. When they become ambassadors of the change effort, the change spreads.

The existing culture of any given school did not develop overnight, and a new culture will not take hold immediately, either. The process is gradual, with growth

FIGURE 2.2 | The Teacher Buy-In/Buy-Out Continuum

Continuum Position	Behavioral and Attitudinal Traits
Complete Buy-Out (left pole)	Teachers . . . • Have a demeanor ranging from unpleasant to hostile. • Mock the process. • Sabotage other members' efforts. • Exhibit an overt lack of interest and (at times) disrespect. • Are frequently tardy to or absent from meetings. • Make inappropriate jokes. • Withdraw psychologically during meetings. • Frequently and vocally disagree with opinions, suggestions, decisions, and tasks. • Refuse or consistently fail to do anything the team decides.
Skepticism	Teachers . . . • Ask challenging questions, sometimes to derail the meeting. • Make frequent negative comments. • Resent "having" to participate. • Are reluctant to give the work a try.
Compliance	Teachers . . . • Have a standoffish demeanor. • Do only what is required. • Neither impede nor encourage progress. • May be superficially engaged.
Commitment	Teachers . . . • Have an optimistic demeanor. • Have personal "skin in the game" from having volunteered in various capacities. • Ask questions to deepen personal understanding. • Are willing to try any new task or protocol.
Complete Buy-In (right pole)	Teachers . . . • Have an enthusiastic demeanor. • Act as ambassadors for the work of the team. • Aspire to leadership roles in the team. • Frequently volunteer. • Show deep engagement in the work of the PLC.

spurts here and there and occasional plateaus as well. Principals and teacher leaders must keep this in mind as they persist in chiseling away at the status quo and replacing it with effective change. Eventually, the school will reach a point where a critical mass of teachers buy in to and embrace the work. Shortly thereafter, schools reach a "tipping point," as Malcolm Gladwell (2000) calls it, where the cultural change takes firm root and there is no going back to the old culture (see Figure 2.3). I have witnessed this tipping point a number of times, and each time I am in awe at the power of authentic, high-functioning PLCs. Keep the faith. ***Trust the process.***

Moving Toward Buy-In: Factors and Obstacles to Consider

As discussed, getting a faculty or a PLC to the point of 100 percent buy-in is neither the goal nor realistically attainable. And given the fact that the mechanism of buy-in is more a continuum than a light switch, PLCs are in a constant state of *moving toward* buy-in. In the following few sections we'll consider some factors that promote buy-in as well as common obstacles that impede it.

Teacher Readiness

Just as there is a continuum of teacher buy-in, there is a continuum of teacher *readiness* to embrace any significant school change, especially working collaboratively with colleagues in an authentic PLC. Effective principals and PLC facilitators are aware of this, acknowledge it, and respond to different faculty members in kind. Like buy-in, readiness is a changeable quality; where a teacher is today may be different

FIGURE 2.3 | The Tipping Point

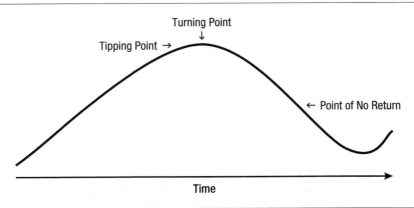

from where she is tomorrow. What is important for school and PLC leaders to keep in mind is that their leadership ought to reflect this and be sufficiently differentiated so that each member of the faculty or PLC is inched along the continuum of readiness one step at a time, without skipping any steps. It is likely that folks will be at different levels of readiness to be part of an authentic PLC, and that is really OK. If we want to prepare a whole faculty for significant change in the school culture, we need to work with teachers *where they are.*

Teacher Comfort Zones

We all have personal comfort zones, and teachers are no exception. For teachers with expansive comfort zones, there is no new idea or way of doing things that they are not willing to try. But most teachers have narrower comfort zones, and their willingness to embrace change is tempered by how that change will affect their professional lives. In my experience, the degree to which change is embraced rarely correlates with the validity of the change in question. Teachers' acceptance of change is a function more of what that change means to them personally than of why the change is a good idea or stands to improve student learning (Evans, 2001). Because of this, emotionally driven arguments in favor of or against change often trump compelling intellectual arguments. This is nothing new; commercial and political advertisers have known it for ages.

The *Groundhog Day* Effect

In the 1993 comedy *Groundhog Day,* actor Bill Murray plays a common man who experiences the same day over and over with only minor differences each time— a scenario that resonates with many veteran teachers. One of the biggest adversaries of school change is the collective institutional memory of similar changes that were attempted in the past, failed, and were quickly abandoned despite well-intentioned administrators' initial enthusiasm and vows that the change was "here to stay." That history stays vivid in the minds of all those teachers who bought in to the idea and who now look back at their trust with scorn and see the energy they expended as a waste of time. Teachers who have been with the school or district for a significant length of time have probably seen this phenomenon repeat itself again and again. Can we really blame these teachers for their skepticism, distrust, and resistance to the new change we are proposing? Why should they believe that somehow this time things will play out differently? Every previously failed initiative contributes to a cumulative reduction in faculty faith that the next one will work. When leaders consider why there may be resistance to this new change—however valid that change is—they should not overlook or dismiss the school's history of fallen initiatives.

The Parking Lot Meeting

Each of us in education has at some point experienced what I call the "Parking Lot Meeting." This is the meeting after the meeting. This is the meeting that spontaneously erupts as teachers walk to their cars after the faculty (or PLC, or team) meeting has adjourned. This is the informal meeting where teachers say what they *really* think, where dissenting opinions not expressed at the actual meeting freely fly. The Parking Lot Meeting can have a significant negative effect on the opinions and attitudes of the teachers who are present, even those who are passive attendees. It has a similar effect on the general faculty as well, all without the principal or PLC coach ever being aware. Thus, it is imperative that PLC facilitators be transparent in all meetings, embracing and addressing disagreement, inviting teachers' voice, and creating an atmosphere of trust and safety where dissenting opinions may be offered and heard without judgment. This is easier said than done, but this dynamic is an essential characteristic of authentic and high-functioning PLCs. The pay-off is substantial: PLC meetings in which teachers have a voice and may freely disagree with the majority opinion without facing scorn or judgment are rarely followed by a Parking Lot Meeting.

Teachers and Change: A Historical Metaphor

The authors of an article for the *Journal of Research for Educational Leaders* (Shanks, Beck, & Staloch, 2006) have come up with an interesting and apt metaphor for teachers and change. They compare types of teachers facing school change to the types of settlers and explorers during the 19th century westward expansion of the United States (see Figure 2.4).

FIGURE 2.4 | Historical Metaphor: Teachers and Change

Explorers | These teachers are the unabashed leaders, willing to try anything at any time without knowledge that it will work.

Pioneers | These teachers will try new initiatives and influence others to try them—*after* someone has demonstrated success with the initiatives. They are cautious leaders.

Settlers | These teachers will follow the leaders once there are enough people engaging in and succeeding with a new initiative.

Pessimistic storytellers | These teachers quietly stay behind and do what has always "worked for me." They resist change themselves but have no problem witnessing other people trying new things.

Keepers-of-the-nightmares | These teachers not only resist change, but they will also do everything possible to sabotage the change for others. They live for "I told you so" moments when new initiatives don't go as planned.

The distribution of teachers across these five types is a bell curve: most teachers tend to be settlers when facing school change, particularly cultural change. There tend to be very few explorers; even teachers in leadership positions tend to be pioneers rather than explorers. Equally few in number are the keepers-of-the-nightmares. Teacher leaders who are at the helm of implementing school change sometimes think there are more keepers-of-the-nightmares among the faculty than there actually are.

My aim in including these classifications here is not to label individual teachers but to raise awareness that, during any period of significant school change, not all teachers start out at the same place—and wherever they may start out is not a permanent position on the continuum of teacher buy-in.

Building Teacher Trust and Buy-In

There is a difference between *trust* and *buy-in*, although the two terms are sometimes conflated in education. *Buy-in* refers to the extent to which a teacher believes in the worthiness of the PLC's mission, tasks, and processes. Teachers deciding whether to buy in to these ask themselves questions such as *Is this worth my time and energy? How effective is this likely to be? Do I agree with the fundamental and underlying values of the work? Will this initiative have faded away by this time next year?*

Trust, in a broad sense, refers to the extent to which a teacher believes in the judgment, integrity, and track record of the people with whom he or she works. Questions related to trust include *Does this person have a history of being dependable and honest? If I do as she suggests, is she unlikely to betray me? Is she likely to follow up on her end with what she has promised? Will I be protected if I am vulnerable or take risks? Do I have faith in her judgment?*

Of course, there are other forms of trust that are required in authentic PLCs: trust in the process, trust in other members, trust in the protocols, trust in ourselves, and so forth. But many of these forms of trust still come down to trusting the person at the helm, the facilitator of the PLC. If we trust her, we'll give the protocol a try, and we'll believe that we can do things we never thought we were capable of.

Trust and buy-in, although distinct, are interconnected. Each requires the other. Each begets the other. So how do we build trust and buy-in? I find it illuminating to think in terms of *trust capital*: the facilitator's relationship with each member of the PLC has a kind of "trust account," and nearly everything that happens at the facilitator's hands makes either a deposit to or a withdrawal from this trust account. A facilitator can take specific actions to build trust capital (see Figure 2.5, p. 28). Growth may be slow at first, but as PLC members consistently receive small deposits into their trust accounts, their trust in the facilitator and in the work itself increases. The opposite is also true: regular withdrawals from trust accounts

FIGURE 2.5 | Depositing Capital into the Trust Account

To increase trust . . .

- Be transparent from the very beginning.
- Acknowledge and respect individual teachers' readiness.
- Identify, meet, and balance individual and group needs.
- Ask people what they think.
- Expect buy-in at every meeting.
- Debrief everything.

- Address chronic tardiness.
- Never ignore sarcasm or other negative comments.
- Recognize silent transformations (in readiness, trust, risk taking, and buy-in).
- Practice differentiated facilitation.
- Don't be "knowlier than thou."
- Model being vulnerable and taking risks.

can reach a critical point at which the trust relationship is too eroded for the team to operate at a functional level.

Although it may have been a fun thing to do at summer camp, *you don't build trust from doing trust falls.* At its core, trust comes when we let ourselves be vulnerable and take risks—and come out the other side in one piece. Trust results from the experience of venturing out onto the "skinny branches" and still feeling safe enough to bare our teacher souls and admit our frailties—and have those met with understanding and support rather than evaluation and judgment. Trust also emerges from the experience of watching others bare *their* teacher souls in a safe, supportive, and honest environment and witnessing them actually being helped by the PLC. If I am a teacher who feels trepidation about presenting my work to the PLC, but I witness another teacher doing so and being helped rather than judged, I might decide to bring my own work to a future meeting. Unfortunately, this notion also works in reverse: if such an experience is ever perilous and doesn't end well, not only will the presenting teacher be unlikely to bring future work, but so, too, will the rest of the PLC. If a child falls during a summer camp trust-fall activity, not only will he never take a turn in the future, but neither will the next kid in line.

The best way a facilitator can build trust in a PLC is to consistently run authentic meetings relevant to the work of its members. When teachers start to see a difference in their own classrooms, in the classrooms of their colleagues, and in the collective learning of all their students, trust skyrockets—and so does buy-in. With every meaningful meeting the PLC has, trust among its members and buy-in to the work increase. There is no sales pitch mightier than productive meetings.

With that central tenet in mind, facilitators should also strive for the following principles: safety first, facilitative transparency, responsive facilitation, voice and choice, following up, differentiated facilitation, and team-centric facilitation. Read on.

Safety First

Teachers who take part in an authentic PLC are agreeing to be part of an environment in which vulnerability and risk taking are commonplace. For PLC members to bare their teacher souls in sharing their work or the work of their students, a culture of safety must be in place. Safety is not an option. We cannot ask teachers to show vulnerability unless we insulate them from the possibility of a bad experience. This is paramount to everything that happens in the PLC, and it is the facilitator's job to ensure safety for all teachers all of the time without compromise.

This is not to say that honest feedback and critical opinions should be withheld; on the contrary, safety is important precisely *because* honest feedback and critical opinions are part of the culture and, in many ways, operationally define *authentic*. If we only praised and celebrated one another's work, we wouldn't need to concern ourselves with safety. We need more provisions for safety out on the skinny branches.

When we give colleagues feedback, what we say and how we say it matter greatly, and it is the facilitator who is the referee of such feedback. A critical comment expressed with good intentions can be received badly. On more than one occasion, I have asked a member of my PLC to reword his or her comment because I believed it was too harsh or would be interpreted as too harsh by the teacher whose work we were examining. Intercepting such comments as soon as they are offered, before the presenting teacher has had a chance to respond, promotes a sense of safety. Sometimes teachers with the very best ideas and opinions are the very worst at expressing them in an effective, safe manner. As facilitators, we must keep our eyes and ears open at all times and respond with diligence when necessary. Chapter 7 addresses this issue in greater detail.

Facilitative Transparency

Transparency is crucial for building trust—and if facilitators are running authentic PLCs, they have nothing to fear by being transparent. After all, when facilitators prioritize the needs of the PLC over their own personal needs and wants, the decisions they make will always reflect what is best for the team. As such, it is best practice to be transparent about how any decisions have been made and what factors contributed to those decisions. Operating this way shows respect for the members of the PLC and models a degree of vulnerability that we want to establish in the culture of the team. Sometimes, transparency manifests itself in the facilitator's comfort with admitting that he or she doesn't know the answer to a question or isn't exactly sure how a new protocol goes. A culture of transparency often grows from the facilitator's demonstration of this principle. If the time comes when the facilitator needs to have a heart-to-heart with the members of the team, it's easier to do when he or she has first established a history of transparency.

Responsive Facilitation

Good teachers are attuned to the minute-by-minute effect of their instruction on the learners before them and are able to tweak their instruction in real time based on learner responses. In *How Teachers Can Turn Data into Action*, I use the phrase *bat teaching* to refer to this continuous cycle of sending out instructional probes that result in student responses, which in turn result in slight modifications to instruction—much like the echolocation signals bats use to navigate.

Effective facilitators operate in the same manner. They maintain a continual heightened awareness of the psychosocial state of PLC members and make micro-adjustments to what they are doing as they lead their teams in any given task. Like the effective teacher's tweaks to instruction, these responses are small, subtle, and seamless; they are more a part of the fabric of their facilitation than conscious acts of effort. This type of facilitation is known as *responsive facilitation*. The self-evaluation instrument in Figure 2.6 will help facilitators reflect on their progress in becoming responsive facilitators.

FIGURE 2.6 | Considerations for Responsive Facilitation

Facilitation is a crucial part of any kind of collaborative work. A responsive facilitator has to keep many things in mind as he or she supports the work of a collaborative group. The following list is intended as both a general reminder of important skills and a checklist of areas one might want to focus on for personal growth.

A responsive facilitator has to . . .

   ___ 1. Pay attention to group dynamics all the time—body language, who's speaking and who's not, tone of voice, reactions between group members, secondary agendas, and judgmental comments;

   ___ 2. Pay attention to inclusion of all members;

   ___ 3. Attend to agreed-upon group norms, adding new norms as needed for productive group work;

   ___ 4. Be able to help a group figure out what it needs, or . . .

   ___ 5. Figure out what a group needs if it can't, give guidance, and then . . .

   ___ 6. Be able to change the agenda to meet the group needs without losing sight of the purpose and goals of the activity, workshop, or work session;

   ___ 7. Be able to distinguish between one's own agenda and the agenda of the group;

   ___ 8. Have a way to identify oneself in the role of facilitator, teacher, or person when the roles change and to let the group know (e.g., literally wearing one of three different hats for each role);

   ___ 9. Know when you are stumped and get help from a colleague or ask the group where to go now (transparent facilitation often works well)—it is important not to appear to be an expert when stuck;

FIGURE 2.6 | Considerations for Responsive Facilitation (continued)

___ 10. Recognize when the whole group, including the facilitator, is "stuck," and put the issue or dilemma in the "parking lot" for later when there's been time for reflection and distance, and move on;

___ 11. Be able to step back—get some distance—when you feel yourself being emotionally drawn into difficult group dynamics;

___ 12. Own up to goofs and misperceptions—they are usually great opportunities for learning, and you provide modeling;

___ 13. Resist taking things personally. Groups or individuals sometimes vent their frustration, anger, and fears on the facilitators. That can be a sign of dissonance and usually means progress and change. Take several deep breaths;

___ 14. Work for balance between process and content, but give precedence to process over content when you have to choose. Safe, bonded communities of learners have a higher learning curve;

___ 15. Celebrate when groups move from pseudo-community to the beginnings of real community in a longer workshop. Little of substance can happen in a pseudo-community where everyone is being "nice." This change often occurs on the third day people are together. The passage is often stormy, comes at unexpected moments over surprising issues, and sometimes involves tears, anger, fear, guilt, or other strong emotions. Facilitating a group through this passage can be tricky work. It is here where a facilitator has to distinguish between the growth of a community through the intended goals and purpose—and therapy. Facilitators are not therapists, and it is vital not to cross that line, however fuzzy it seems at times;

___ 16. Keep a sense of humor! Everyone is human and can make any number of amazing mistakes as well as bring memorable insight and wisdom. Laughing together is a gift and helps keep perspective.

Scoring Guide

4 = I find (will find) this easy to do.
3 = I find this somewhat easy to do.
2 = I find this somewhat hard to do.
1 = I find this hard to do.

Activity

1. Quietly and individually, participants score themselves on each item (see scoring guide above).
2. Then each participant chooses two high-scoring items (with a score of 3 or 4) and two low-scoring items (with a score of 1 or 2).
3. In turn, each participant shares his or her two high and two low items, with a brief explanation for each. Other members in the group practice asking follow-up questions.
4. Debrief.

Source: National School Reform Faculty (NSRF). Special permission has been received to reproduce this checklist. The NSRF offers more than 300 protocols and activities, plus coaches' trainings to use materials most effectively, improving teaching practice and student achievement. See http://www.nsrfharmony.org or call 812-330-2702 for details.

Voice and Choice

Few things engender buy-in (and, to some extent, trust) as much as giving teachers a voice in decisions affecting the direction the team will take. In cases where it's not practical or advisable to give PLC members full decision power, offering them options to choose from runs a close second. Does this principle not also work well with students in the classroom—even the most challenging students? When students have a say in their learning, they are much more likely to be engaged with it. Teachers are not different in this regard, especially in school environments where top-down decisions and initiatives are commonplace. See Figure 2.7 for some do's and don'ts to consider when giving PLC members voice and choice.

Authentic facilitation requires leaders to continually balance being in control with giving up control. Giving participants in the PLC voice and choice is an example of giving up control in a way that not only produces surprisingly good decisions, but also heightens members' ownership of and commitment to the work of the PLC.

FIGURE 2.7 | A Guide to Giving PLC Members Voice and Choice

DO . . .	DON'T . . .
• Be willing to go with (or seriously consider) the team's choice. • Actively listen to the team's input. • Ask yourself, "Can the team decide this, or must I?" • Trust the team's decisions and opinions and believe they are made in earnest. • Hear out opinions that are contrary to your own. Remember, you asked for them.	• Give the team choices unless you can live with your least favorite one on the list. • Ask for team members' opinions if you've already made up your mind. • Ask your team to make a decision you're avoiding making yourself. • Be afraid to change your opinion on something based on the team's input. • Take too long to reach a decision. Giving voice and choice can sometimes slow down the process of deciding the next best avenue for the team.

Following Up

I am frequently taken aback by how shocked teachers and teams are when I follow up, often days later, with something I said I would do or look into. Judging from my experience, it is clear that this must not be the norm. A successful way to build trust with your team is to follow this simple, rather obvious, maxim: ***do what you say you're going to do.*** When you follow up on things that come up in a meeting—things that are important to team members—it sends a clear message that you are serious about the work and about taking care of your team. It doesn't matter so much if you think the issues are important; if something is important to the team, then it becomes corollarily important to you. Following up even on little things builds big gains in trust.

Differentiated Facilitation

When I started teaching in 1980, the dominant instructional method was to teach all kids the same way and leave them to "sink or swim." We shot for the middle and routinely left behind those at the bottom and, to a great extent, those at the top. In the nearly four decades that have passed since then, we have learned a great deal about the different ways that students learn, the different timelines along which they learn, and how to accommodate these differences. Thanks to pioneering educators like Carol Ann Tomlinson, differentiated instruction has become widely practiced—if not quite perfected—in classrooms throughout the United States.

Like students in the classroom, teachers can vary significantly in their background knowledge and experience, their learning and communication preferences, their readiness to accept challenge or risk, and their interests and stakes in education. We are not aiming to build Stepford PLCs; each PLC comprises *individuals.* To honor these individuals' differences and facilitate accordingly is to have the most productive, most cohesive band of teachers who function at the highest levels for the good of their students.

Differentiated facilitation happens continually, every time teachers meet as a PLC. Facilitators put forethought into which kinds of questions are appropriate to ask different members, and they temper their opinions, feedback, and challenges according to the recipient. As is the case in the classroom, the best way to differentiate is to really know the individuals present and use that knowledge to capitalize on strengths, avoid stirring up insecurities, and appreciate and validate what each member brings to the team.

The following Fly on the Wall shows how Angie differentiates her facilitation in responding to two PLC members' noncompliance with a team agreement.

What Happened

At a previous PLC meeting, teachers on the 8th grade social studies team created a short writing assignment to give in each of their classes and drafted a short rubric for scoring the papers. They also agreed to bring five unscored representative student papers to the next PLC meeting. As the follow-up meeting starts and Angie asks members to take out their samples, it becomes clear that neither Bruce nor Evelyn has brought any student papers.[1]

Angie is taken aback by this but maintains a calm demeanor.

Angie: Bruce?[2]

Bruce: I completely forgot to do this with my classes. I apologize.

Evelyn: I don't have any papers, either. I did give students the assignment, but I must not have been clear about what I expected, because the work was really bad—not worth bringing to the meeting.

Angie: I want to apologize for the next five minutes of this meeting to Cassandra and Devin, who brought student samples. Bruce, I'm going to be completely honest with you. It's not OK to forget to do something we all agreed to do. It's disrespectful to the people who did do it and to the process as a whole. And even though you're present for this meeting, you stand to get less out of it. That's not fair to you or your students.[3]

Bruce: I know. You're right. I guess I thought my kids might have trouble with this, and if they're not ready, then I shouldn't do it.

Angie: That's understandable, Bruce.[4] That's relevant information that's important for us to know as a team. In retrospect, when might have been a better time to share that information?

Bruce: I guess at the last meeting when we planned this.

Angie: (to the whole team) If any one of us is not comfortable with something we are deciding as a team, we need to say so right away, during the planning stage. If Bruce had shared this about his kids, we could have discussed as a team more appropriate alternatives to that assignment. We're still learning as a team, and I'm still learning as your facilitator.[5] I hope we all think about this and remember this the next time we plan to do something in each of our classes.

Evelyn: I was kind of in the same boat. I thought my kids might have trouble with this, and they did.

Angie: Even though your kids had trouble, Evelyn, I still think that it would have been valuable to bring the papers to this meeting—in some sense, *especially* because they had trouble.[6] The purpose of this meeting is to analyze the work the students produced, discuss the strong points and the gaps in the assignment itself, and take corrective action to assist students who did struggle with it—in all of our classes—so that we can use their work to gauge what we could have done differently and, more important, what we should do next. Not having your students' work leaves them out of this conversation, in a sense.[7] If we only discuss the students who are successful, then those who need our support are underrepresented in this discussion. Does this make sense?

Evelyn: Yeah, it does. Should I go get the papers right now?

Angie: If you're comfortable sharing them, then yes, I think it would be great to have them on the table for all of us to benefit from.

Cassandra: I had a good half-dozen kids who did really poorly on this as well. I agree that it is important to include them in the discussion of what's next. Evelyn, I'm happy that you're going to get the papers because I think we can all help those kids and not just leave you with that responsibility.[8]

What's Worth Noting

[1]This is the quintessential dread of every PLC facilitator. There are a variety of reasons why this happens; the solution requires careful consideration of possible reasons in each case.

[2]In all likelihood, Bruce didn't give the assignment because it wasn't a priority to him. For him, the pain of assigning the paper was greater than the pain of facing his team without the papers. Evelyn, by contrast, gave the assignment and felt considerable trepidation sharing the poor results with her team. Her pain was in facing the shame (in her mind) of sharing such bad work, probably assuming that the work of the students in the other classes was good. Although neither Bruce nor Evelyn admitted to weighing the pros and cons of giving the assignment, both made such an assessment, if not at the conscious level.

[3]Angie has assessed the reasons why Bruce and Evelyn failed to bring the student samples and reacts accordingly: she takes a certain admonishing posture toward Bruce, and she reassures Evelyn that it's OK to bring disappointing student work to the group.

(continued)

[4]Angie also validates Bruce's reason for not giving the assignment. Without offering some validation, any admonishments are likely to fall on deaf ears and shut Bruce down. She doesn't want that.

[5]It is important to show humility and vulnerability as a facilitator. Angie does so here, which softens the negativity being experienced by the group and boosts optimism for future meetings.

[6]Again, Angie reassures Evelyn.

[7]This is a powerful rationale that Evelyn, in her nurturing way, can identify with.

[8]Cassandra picks up on Angie's attempt to assure Evelyn and corroborates the sentiment.

One protocol I have developed for use in the early stages of building an authentic PLC is the Irks & Quirks Protocol (formerly known as the Peeves & Traits Protocol). It is simple to use, requires no more than 15–20 minutes, and brings to the surface things that are important to know about the members of a PLC. The steps are outlined in Figure 2.8.

Team-Centric Facilitation

It goes without saying that facilitators must always keep what is best for the team in the front of their minds. Although it is sometimes difficult to do, they must put their own needs, preferences, and personal goals aside and **lead the team for the team.** This team-centric facilitation also applies to instances when a particular member of the PLC is dominating the group to serve his or her own interests or agenda. In cases like this, the facilitator must stand up to the individual member and reset the focus of the meeting to what is best for the team and, ultimately, what is best for students. **There is learning in the balance.** A few questions help the resetting process: *What is best for the team right now? Is the path we're on and where we seem to be heading likely to result in good for the whole PLC?*

When a facilitator consistently acts in the best interest of the team, it becomes clear to team members that the facilitator is putting the PLC's needs above his or her own, and it perpetuates a culture in which this disposition is adopted by the rest of the team. It reinforces the notion that modeling a desired behavior is better than proselytizing about the merits of the behavior.

There's a saying I heard years ago relating to the demands placed on teachers in the pervasive climate of high-stakes testing: teachers don't tire if their scores

FIGURE 2.8 | Irks and Quirks Protocol*

Time: 15 minutes

I. Each participant receives an index card. On one side of the card, participants write *one* pet peeve they have regarding working in groups or at teacher meetings. They begin their pet peeve with the phrase *It burns my butt when* . . . . (e.g., "It burns my butt when people come late to meetings," "It burns my butt when people are interrupted during discussions," or "It burns my butt when one person does all the talking."). (3 minutes)

II. On the other side of the card, participants write *one* trait about themselves that everyone in the group should know to best work with them in a group setting. They begin their trait with the phrase *One thing you all should know about me is* . . . . (e.g., "One thing you all should know about me is that my silence is not due to disinterest; I just need processing time," "One thing you all should know about me is I get excited during discussions, and sometimes people are put off by my enthusiasm," or "One thing you all should know about me is I am very visual and need to see what we're discussing on chart paper or the interactive whiteboard."). (3 minutes)

III. Participants share both sides of their cards in volunteer order **without discussion** (or elaborating on the card). (5 minutes)

IV. *The debrief.* The team members reflect aloud on the experience they have just shared. (4 minutes)

*Originally titled "Peeves and Traits" until Grapple participant Justine Szymala came up with this better name.

Source: Irks and Quirks is a pre-activity for setting up norms in teacher groups developed by Daniel R. Venables. From D. Venables, *The Practice of Authentic PLCs: A Guide to Effective Teacher Teams,* Corwin, 2011. Copyright 2011 by Corwin. Adapted with permission.

are higher. This sentiment has an analogue in the world of authentic PLCs. Being a member of an authentic PLC requires hard work, and it's not always smooth sailing. Facilitating one is even harder. But the rewards—both personal and professional—are truly satisfying, and it's harder to tire of the work and the energy expenditure when we really see the difference it makes for kids. I have seen it up close and personal in many schools, and I will never tire of this cause.

Trust and buy-in form the bedrock of everything we build in an authentic PLC. Any time spent cultivating these two is never time wasted, and it is impossible to have too much of either. They take time to develop but, once established, do not crumble or dissolve easily. In the next chapter I discuss some more advanced aspects of facilitating an authentic PLC—none of which is possible to achieve without a foundation of trust and buy-in.

3 | FACILITATION 201

Being a skillful facilitator of an authentic PLC takes a great deal of courage. It requires courage not to take it personally when team members are unhappy with how a meeting is going or openly express resistance to what you're trying to do. It takes courage to face naysayers head-on, with respect and honesty. It takes courage to push team members when they are taking the easy way out in their discussion of difficult issues. It takes courage to disagree with a member who isn't getting it, when you privately feel thrilled that she is even participating. It is so much easier not to say anything. It takes real courage to speak up, allowing yourself to march indomitably outside your comfort zone and onto the skinny branches because you know it's best for the team (and therefore best for the kids).

In this chapter, we will drill deeper and examine the more complex components of authentic facilitation. What I refer to as the "heavy lifting" of facilitation requires the PLC leader to question team members skillfully, facilitate peer feedback, manage intellectual conflict and other team growth spurts, balance the need to be in control with the need to relinquish control, and share the facilitation load. Read on for strategies to effectively manage these crucial elements of authentic facilitation.

The Art and Importance of Questioning

Like good teaching, good facilitation requires us to be skilled in the art of asking questions. The following sections explore various purposes and strategies for effective questioning.

Getting Teachers' Opinions

Working in a collaborative teacher team requires us to acknowledge that important conversations around teaching and learning necessarily encompass differences in opinions, experiences, priorities, and assumptions. When teachers in an authentic PLC are willing to come to the table to discuss important matters regarding teaching and learning, it is essential that their opinions be solicited and listened to. Doing so can draw out even the most recalcitrant member. No teacher has ever been bothered by someone asking for his or her opinion; generally, there is no shortage of opinions among teachers. Asking teachers for their opinions isn't just good form; it elicits a better product, result, solution, or decision than if we rely only on our own opinions or on the unsolicited opinions of the more vocal PLC members. I am reminded of David Weinberger's (2011) adage that "The smartest person in the room is the room itself."

At every reasonable opportunity, the facilitator should solicit the team's opinions. But asker beware: if we ask people for their opinions, we have to listen to the responses and consider them seriously as we decide how to move forward.

Creating a Culture of Asking Rather Than Telling

An ingrained belief in most teacher cultures is that the person leading the meeting generally has the most knowledge about any topic the group might discuss. Teachers in meetings tend to look to the leader for information, insights, and guidance. We know, however, from the research of Michael Fullan (2011, 2014, 2016) and Doug Reeves (2009) that this authoritarian model of leadership is of limited effectiveness. More effective than telling teachers what we think, what we would do, what we value, and what we prefer is asking them what *they* think, what *they* would do, what *they* value, and what *they* prefer. There is a simple psychology at play here: teachers who are asked what they would do are more likely to do it. Further, teachers' answers to questions about what would be best for students or what action they should take are likely to be consistent with what they perceive the group leader wants to hear. This may sound a bit like trickery on the facilitator's part, but the fact is, seeking insights and advice from teachers truly does give them voice and choice; it's just that the resulting groupthink overwhelmingly skews in the direction of actually helping kids learn, even when that means some sacrifice on the part of the teachers.

Pushing the Conversation to a Deeper Level

Effective facilitators don't ask questions purely for the purpose of soliciting teachers' opinions. Sometimes a facilitator may pose a question with the goal of deepening the discussion or gearing it more specifically toward instruction. These questions most often are follow-up questions to a comment from the group. Examples include *What would happen if . . . ? Which standards are addressed by the written component of this?* and *What convinced you that this is true?* The last question is a safe and diplomatic way of asking for evidence to support an unsubstantiated statement. Figure 3.1 (see p. 40) includes additional question stems and examples.

Challenging Conventional Thinking

Let's face it: conventional thinking leads to conventional teaching, which, although not altogether a bad thing, leads to conventional (read: slow) rates of growth.

FIGURE 3.1 | PLC Coach's Guide to Asking Deeper Questions

The role of the PLC coach or facilitator involves much more than simply delineating the agenda or leading PLC members through the steps of a timely protocol. Although these tasks have their place and are part of the PLC coach's "job description," they do not actually lead the PLC to do work that has a significant effect on student learning. To truly improve the work of the collective PLC and of individual teachers, PLC coaches must make a habit of asking probing, difficult questions.

Without addressing deeper questions, the team is just a group of teachers who go through a series of motions that have been approved as proper practices of a PLC, but who do nothing to improve student learning. The last thing busy teachers need is to participate in meetings that, in the end, do nothing of real significance to foster their students' learning.

I developed this guide, which draws from resources from the National School Reform Faculty's "Pocket Guide to Probing Questions," to help PLC coaches go deeper and push their PLC members to go deeper so that they can make significant strides in instructional improvement. If PLCs are to do authentic, substantive work, PLC coaches must not only ask deeper questions and prompt PLC members to think on a deeper level but also relentlessly pursue asking these deeper questions. In my experience, this does not happen unless the PLC coach is aware of the importance of asking deeper questions and knows what such questions might look like.

Deeper questions . . .

- Are general and widely useful, often transcending the content of the moment.
- Allow for multiple responses.
- Help create a paradigm shift in the thinking of individuals and teams.
- Empower individuals and teams to think more expansively about a topic, an issue, or a dilemma.
- Avoid yes or no responses.
- Elicit slow, thoughtful responses.
- Move thinking from reaction to reflection, from being reactive to being proactive.
- Encourage taking another party's perspective.

Some general question stems that help push deeper thinking include the following:

- Why do you think this is the case?
- What would have to change in order for . . . ?
- What do you feel is right in your gut?
- What do you wish . . . ?
- What's another way you might . . . ?
- What would it look like if . . . ?
- What do you think would happen if . . . ?
- How was [ABC] different from [XYZ]?
- What sort of effect do you think [ABC] would have on [XYZ]?
- What criteria did you use to . . . ?
- When have you done/experienced something like this before?
- What might you see happening in your classroom if . . . ?
- How did you determine that [XYZ] was best?
- What is your hunch about . . . ?
- What was your intention when . . . ?
- What do you assume to be true about . . . ?
- What is the connection between [ABC] and [XYZ]?

FIGURE 3.1 | PLC Coach's Guide to Asking Deeper Questions (continued)

- What if the opposite were true? What would happen?
- How might your assumptions about [*ABC*] have influenced how you were thinking about [*XYZ*]?
- Why is this such a dilemma for you?

Some questions that help push data conversations include the following:

- What do you think that implies?
- Do you think we have evidence to support that statement? Where?
- Can you point to specific evidence?
- Why? How do you know?
- Do you think this is something that is systemic or specific to particular student populations?
- What do you think we should do to address that?
- What are the big issues here, as opposed to the secondary or ancillary issues?
- Can we see root causes, based on the evidence, that give rise to secondary symptoms in the issues we're seeing? What are the root causes?

When team members address deeper questions, important truths about instructional practice come to light. It's not that teachers have been hiding anything; it's more that they have not spent adequate time really looking at what they do and, more important, at the effect of their actions on student learning. It is the PLC coach's job to push this kind of questioning so that these truths bubble to the surface during discourse. The questions and question stems in this guide can help.

Source: Developed by D. R. Venables, Center for Authentic PLCs (www.authenticplcs.com), drawing from resources from NSRF's "Pocket Guide to Probing Questions." Special permission has been received to reproduce text from the National School Reform Faculty. See http://www.nsrfharmony.org or call 812-330-2702 for more resources and to learn about coaches' training to use NSRF resources most effectively.

If we want to do the best possible work for *our* kids—not the conventional kids of 20 years ago—we have to think in new ways that reflect the world in which they (and we) reside. For example, is memorizing state capitals or the types of clouds as important as learning how to read Facebook posts with skepticism and sift through the preponderance of nonsense on the Internet that masquerades as fact? Facilitating an authentic PLC means fostering teachers' willingness to challenge traditional mores of teaching, learning, and curriculum. Even when we are bound by conventional content standards, we are not required to design conventional curricula and lesson plans. As long as they align with the standards, we can explore ways of learning and teaching in unconventional contexts.

Exploring Dissenting Opinions

Generally, when a member of a PLC dares to offer an opinion that differs significantly from the rest of the team's, either one of two things is true: (1) the team has established a foundation of trust and a culture of risk taking that embraces such differences of opinion, or (2) the dissenting member has that personality type that drives him or her to disagree with everything for the sport of it. In either case, effective facilitators never dismiss such opinions. On the contrary, they dig deeper into the opinions by asking the dissenters why they believe this or that to be true. This serves two purposes. First, as long as the facilitator's inquiry is sincere and non-judgmental, the dissenter feels validated in his or her opinion. To be responded to is to have been heard. Second, the facilitator and the rest of the team gain a clearer understanding of why the dissenter feels the way he or she does and where his or her opinion is coming from. Teachers make assumptions about teaching and learning and students all the time; it sometimes takes a dissenting opinion and an inquiry about it to allow those assumptions to bubble to the surface. Such an understanding can only strengthen the team, even if other members are not persuaded to change their minds about the issue.

Drawing Minority or Silent Voices into the Conversation

Silence can be a good thing in an authentic PLC, indicating deep thinking and reflection. As I mentioned in Chapter 1, I can often determine how seasoned a PLC facilitator is by his or her comfort with silence in the group.

But there is also a more destructive side of silence. This is the silence of members who do not agree with the rest of the team but do not feel comfortable sharing their opinions. There are several possible reasons for this state of affairs:

- The general safety of team members has been compromised.
- The group has a history of invalidating dissenting opinions.
- The most vocal members have dominated the team into submission.
- The facilitator has misinterpreted silence as agreement.

Silence rarely implies agreement. More often, silent members are not on board with the sentiments of the rest of their colleagues. To assume that their silence means concurrence is like assuming that all the quiet kids in class are understanding the lesson. Experienced teachers know that some degree of unrest lies beneath the silence in many cases. Effective facilitators are able to draw out silent teachers without putting them on the spot. This can be tricky; asking people by name what they think can sometimes lead to further withdrawal. Often, saying "I'd like to hear from somebody who hasn't weighed in on this yet" or "I'd like to hear the rest of the group's thoughts on what Ms. Baker just shared" is enough. Sometimes, coupling these kinds of statements with a direct (but welcoming) glance to the silent parties is all they need to be prodded into offering their thoughts. And often, they have really thoughtful comments—they just needed a bit of cajoling in a safe zone.

Giving Voice to the Naysayers—While Holding Them Accountable

There is a difference between a dissenter and a naysayer. The dissenter has a different opinion from those being discussed and deserves a place at the table. Often, healthy disagreement is what provides the traction necessary to move the wheel of improvement. The naysayer, by contrast, is a self-appointed contrarian or malcontent who does not constructively contribute to team discourse but, rather, impedes progress, often because of his or her personal disdain for change. In almost all cases, the naysayer is motivated by what is best for him- or herself, not by what is best for students. As such, the naysayer is difficult to deal with; logic and sound reasoning do little to modify his or her opinions.

Still, like the dissenter, the naysayer needs to voice his or her opinions, however destructive they may be. Ignoring this member seems to fuel his or her unpleasantness and make facilitation more difficult with each successive meeting. Letting the naysayer air his or her concerns, self-serving though they may be, permits facilitators to respond to them in a way that may, in the end, be constructive. We're not letting the naysayer off the hook; quite the reverse—we are holding this team member accountable for what he or she says by asking follow-up questions and pursuing his or her line of reasoning to its logical (or nonsensical) end. Once this happens, the time invested often pays off in less naysaying and sabotaging of ideas in future meetings. It's a worthy investment.

Candor with Care: Facilitating Peer Feedback

Although administrator feedback on teacher instruction has a powerful (if infrequent) influence on teachers' practice (Clark & Duggins, 2016), there is no disputing the fact that peer feedback is the lifeblood of significant instructional improvement. Without it, and notwithstanding administrator feedback, teachers are left on their own to reflect on and assess the efficacy of their lessons or learning activities. With peer feedback—and its helpful neighbor, suggestions—teachers can expedite the process of revising lessons and other teacher work and improve the quality of those changes.

Discussions in which teachers offer feedback and suggestions to a colleague are among the most important but delicate conversations that happen in authentic PLCs. Long before a team can engage in discussions of this nature, it needs to build a bedrock of trust and respect and become acclimated to the many processes used in authentic PLCs. ***Build the team before you need it*** is not just a slogan; trust is absolutely vital before team members can exchange feedback in any meaningful way.

Part of slaying the feedback dragon, so to speak, is for facilitators to be upfront and transparent about the nature of giving and receiving feedback. Facilitators should acknowledge to PLC members that traditional teacher cultures have not allowed for a structure in which feedback can be safe, honest, and given in the spirit of helping the teacher whose work the team is reviewing. PLC members should also know that it is difficult both to give and to receive feedback, but it is of paramount importance to the PLC's overarching goal: individually and collectively improving instruction for students. A PLC is greater than the sum of its parts; when its members engage in peer feedback, teachers' work can rise to new levels in a way that could never result from working in isolation. But teachers need to know right from the start that the work is difficult and delicate. Protocols help smooth the path for the facilitator and the rest of the team; we'll delve more deeply into these in Part 2 of this book.

The quality and depth of peer feedback matter greatly. Superficial feedback hurts the team. It says that we are afraid or otherwise too uncomfortable to give honest feedback. It says that we don't care enough about the work to give substantive feedback. It says that we don't give *real* feedback in our culture. Feedback can help a teacher (and therefore the team) only if it is sincere and thoughtful and pushes all members to think deeply about the work. In *The Practice of Authentic PLCs,* I write,

> When our interests as givers of cool feedback [i.e., feedback that points out gaps or possible problems with the work] are the interests of the presenting teacher, she is likely to appreciate our cool feedback. PLC coaches should impress upon group members that by <u>not</u> offering cool feedback, they are being *disrespectful* to the presenting teacher, as if to say that the teacher's work isn't important enough to think deeply about and offer suggestions for improvement. This is a seismic shift in thinking about feedback for most teachers. It is a shift that in many ways clinically defines an authentic PLC. (Venables, 2011, p. 48)

In my experience working with teacher teams, I have found that *giving* cool feedback is more difficult than *receiving* it. There's a good reason for this. The teacher who is receiving the feedback has volunteered to bring his or her work to be reviewed. The other team members are giving feedback by default; they have not volunteered to do so. For some teachers, giving feedback is quite a discomforting task. With time and practice, however, and as feedback becomes a permanent part of the PLC's culture, all teachers become more comfortable giving feedback. Once the culture takes hold, it is difficult to imagine it any other way.

Managing Intellectual Conflict and Other Growth Spurts

When teachers in a PLC are having a conflicted discussion about some aspect of teaching and learning, it can be difficult for the facilitator to see such open—sometimes heated—disagreement as team growth. Yet that's exactly what it is, provided the following ground rules are in place:

- The conflict stays at an intellectual level; it doesn't get personal.
- All involved parties have equal voice and airtime.
- All involved parties show respect for those with whom they disagree—including respect for their differing opinions and for the rights of all to voice their opinions—and demonstrate a willingness to listen to and consider different positions.
- All positions emanate from a belief in what is best for students.

The facilitator would do well to focus on these ground rules throughout the discussion and chime in with questions or comments only if he or she feels that a ground rule is not being followed. If the facilitator focuses on whether the team is staying true to the ground rules rather than on the content of the discussion, there is a good chance that the disagreement will end well, with the team having undergone a growth spurt. The way a PLC's first few intellectual conflicts go tends to set the stage for future conflicts.

Keep in mind that conflicts that are not managed within the PLC tend to be mismanaged elsewhere. When team members feel uncomfortable openly disagreeing or engaging in intellectual conflict, the conflict doesn't go away; it may rear its ugly head in less appropriate contexts, like in a Parking Lot Meeting. Even if the conflict remains below the surface, the lack of openness leaves dissenting parties operating at future meetings without the knowledge of how the other feels. This lack of operational knowledge hurts the PLC as it engages in subsequent discussions, with or without conflict.

Successfully managed conflict is not the only impetus for team growth. Every opportunity taken to construct community knowledge is a point along the continuum of team unity and experience. As team members engage in productive meetings in which they accomplish real work, their levels of trust and buy-in escalate, and the whole team grows. This surge in team growth, in turn, strengthens trust and buy-in. When a team is off and running on the right track, it becomes a living, breathing organism unto itself, and teacher and student successes start emerging like popcorn popping. As with popcorn, things may be slow to heat up, but once the momentum builds, growth spurts come fast and furious. In the early phases, when it feels like nothing is happening, it's important to **trust the process.** Eventually, the PLC will reap the rewards of its patience and assiduousness.

Balancing Being in Control with Giving Up Control

Teachers who are asked to lead PLCs are often selected by their principals because they have natural leadership qualities. Sometimes teachers are asked because they have an existing leadership role within their grade-level team or department. Although possessing natural leadership abilities is an asset in facilitating authentic PLCs, the type of leadership required for the job often differs from the qualities required by other leadership roles, such as grade-level chair, department chair, or instructional coach. In these other roles, leaders usually set the course for the team and support team members in following it. PLC facilitation is more about setting the course *as* a team, without the facilitator's opinions or preferences weighing more heavily than those of any other member. Once the course is determined, effective PLC facilitators keep team members moving toward their common vision. Every step along the way is decided by the team; the facilitator's principal role is to manage the interpersonal dynamics during team discourse. The facilitator does not force his or her agenda on the team but takes team members through the process of deciding it for themselves. A PLC facilitator is no more responsible for the final product or decision than is any other single member of the team. His or her responsibility is to guide the team to the point where those decisions can be made.

The word *navigator* refers to "a person who coordinates the route or course of a ship, aircraft, or other form of transportation. . . . The navigator's primary responsibility is to be aware of ship or aircraft position at all times" (Wikipedia contributors, 2017). Like a navigator, a PLC facilitator must be aware of his or her "ship's" position at all times. In this context, "position" refers not only to where the PLC is in terms of content and goals but also to its thinking and psycho-emotional state at any given point in time. What is team members' comfort level with the work they're doing *right now*? Are their needs being met individually and collectively? Do they perceive the discussion as safe? Are there any silent dissenting voices? Are team members personally invested in what they're doing, or do they appear to be merely appeasing the facilitator?

Effective facilitators embrace the paradox of being in control and giving up control. They know how to balance these two states and can choose the appropriate position to take in any given situation. There are times when a skillful facilitator does little or no talking but silently leads the team by giving up control and letting the team members grapple with whatever they're discussing. Other times, the facilitator takes the reins to ensure that the group continues productively and safely on task. Knowing when to take control and when to cede it marks a seasoned facilitator. All facilitators can reach this level of skill in time, with practice, perseverance, and reflection.

An example of achieving this balance during a discussion is the facilitator's ability to hold back and let most PLC members share their thoughts and opinions before sharing his or hers. I advise PLC facilitators to share last (or nearly last) 80–90 percent of the time. Going last sends a clear message that the facilitator's opinions are not more important than the other members' opinions. This builds a sense of validation for PLC members and emphasizes that the facilitator's role is to listen, not to know more than everyone else.

During the other 10–20 percent of the time, depending on the nature and content of the discussion, it may be important for the facilitator to share early in the process to set a clear example of the kind of contribution the current protocol calls for, or to model depth of thought to the group. Like students in a classroom, team members will follow the standard set by early contributors. This is particularly important in cases where brevity is the rule. Facilitators can control the length of individuals' contributions by modeling brevity themselves. If the first person who talks goes on and on at length, the rest of the PLC will likely follow suit.

Passing the Facilitator Baton and Cofacilitating

My success as a PLC facilitator and as a trainer of PLC facilitators stems in part from my belief that PLCs are only as effective as the teachers who lead them. This premise—not shared by other popular models of PLCs—drives my energies toward helping teacher leaders get really good at knowing what authentic PLCs do, how they do it, and, most important, how to lead others in doing it. Any discussion of sharing the facilitation role with other members of the PLC must be tempered by this notion: facilitators have been trained or in some other way acquired the skill set necessary to lead authentic PLCs, and the rest of the team has not. Therefore, the short answer to the question *Should we take turns facilitating meetings?* is no.

That said, once a PLC has become seasoned and deeply immersed in the work, it makes sense to share some aspects of facilitation with other members. After all, when leadership is shared, commitment to the PLC is shared. In addition, members of the PLC may need to try their own hands at facilitating parts of the meeting in order to fully appreciate how difficult facilitating can be—especially when they tune in to the nuances of interpersonal team dynamics. Start small by asking for a volunteer to lead a debrief of a protocol or a review of the team's norms. Save the heavy-lifting facilitation, such as leading a protocol for looking at teacher work, for yourself. The stakes are too high to place heavier responsibilities on the shoulders of well-intentioned but untrained teachers. And never pass the baton just to avoid facilitating a task that may be tricky or unpleasant. That's your job; it's what you signed up for. The following Fly on the Wall shows what happens when Angie decides to share the facilitation role with a fellow team member.

FLY ON THE WALL

The Scene:
Sharing the Facilitation Role

What Happened

During the second semester, after the PLC had been working together every week for seven months, Angie decided to share her role as facilitator. At one meeting, she announces this decision and passes out copies of an article on mindfully debriefing PLCs (Venables, 2015b). She tells the team that anyone who might be interested in facilitating the debriefing segment of future PLC meetings needs to read the article to get a better general sense of how to lead a meaningful debrief.[1]

At the beginning of the next meeting, Angie asks if anyone would like to lead the debrief of the protocol they're going to use, the Success Analysis Protocol from the National School Reform Faculty. To no one's surprise, Cassandra volunteers.

Angie facilitates the team as it progresses through the steps of the protocol. When the protocol proper is finished, she says, "OK, let's move to step 8, the debrief. Cassandra?"

All eyes move instantly to Cassandra, who jumps right in:

Cassandra: So, what did you think of this process? And remember, we're going to try to discuss only the process for the next five minutes, not the content. Who would like to go first?[2]

No one responds. Cassandra apparently feels uncomfortable with the silence and hurriedly asks another question before anyone can respond to the first:

Cassandra: Did you like it? Did we go too fast? What would you change about this protocol?[3]

Eventually the team members respond, sharing their thoughts about the protocol. Angie responds to several of Cassandra's questions just as any member of the team would.[4] The entire debrief lasts seven minutes, after which the team adjourns.[5]

What's Worth Noting

[1]Angie accomplishes two things here. First, she sets up any volunteers for success by requiring them to learn more about how to debrief effectively. Second, only team members willing to do the extra work of reading the article are eligible to volunteer. This entails a "skin in the game" investment on the volunteer's part.

[2]Cassandra comes on a bit strong here. It's better to ease in, calmly asking one question.

[3]Too many questions strung together can have the effect of shutting down team responses, not encouraging them.

[4]A nice by-product of sharing the facilitator role is that it can free up the usual facilitator to focus exclusively on content for a change.

[5]Before adjourning, it would have been a good idea for Angie to take a couple of minutes to "debrief the debrief" led by Cassandra. This would have given Angie a chance to highlight strengths and thereby encourage others to follow what Cassandra did well if they facilitate part of a meeting in the future.

An exception to not passing the facilitator baton until the team is well established is when the PLC contains two individuals who have been trained as facilitators. In many regards, this is the ideal scenario to enable a PLC to thrive in a relatively short period. When two qualified facilitators share the role, the workload is cut in half, as are the stress of leading a team and the chance of a meeting not going well. As one cofacilitator leads any given task, his or her partner is there to lend support. This support system also plays out in planning the PLC agendas and debriefing the meetings afterward. To have two facilitators able to discuss how the meeting went translates not only to individual facilitator growth but also to indirect team growth. Facilitators who are not afforded the luxury of having a cofacilitator—as is the case with most PLCs—do not have the opportunity to discuss the nuances of a meeting immediately afterward. Outside of the Coaches' PLC (CPLC)—which may meet only monthly if the school even has one—most schools do not have a structure for this kind of PLC facilitator support. For those lucky enough to have cofacilitators, the facilitator learning curve is expedited, which contributes to the overall health of the PLC.

One word of caution for cofacilitators: it is important to decide on specific facilitator assignments before the meeting. Each segment of the agenda should have a designated *lead facilitator*. The lead facilitator should offer ample opportunities for his or her cofacilitator to share thoughts or make remarks (e.g., "Rachael, do you want to add to that?"), but the role of the non–lead cofacilitator is to stay out of the way and chime in only when invited.

All of the points and ideas raised in this chapter go a long way toward assisting a facilitator in understanding what it takes to effectively lead an authentic PLC. There are a lot of moving parts, to be sure, but knowing how they work together helps the facilitator run the PLC machine smoothly. But what happens when things *don't* run smoothly—when a cog in the wheel is inhibiting forward motion? In Chapter 4, we will take a look at obstacles and add to our tool belt strategies for dealing with them effectively.

4 | NAVIGATING DIFFICULT WATERS

In Chapter 2, we discussed how essential trust and buy-in are to building an authentic PLC. In Chapter 3, we looked at advanced strategies for effective facilitation. We will need to keep both of these in mind as we embark on this chapter, which addresses ways to identify and confront interpersonal obstacles that prevent a team from functioning at a high level and getting real results in student learning.

Dealing with Difficult Dynamics

All PLCs are not created equal. For a variety of reasons, some PLCs are difficult to motivate and facilitate. Sometimes this difficulty stems from a history of conflict between two or more members; other times, lines are drawn by age, experience, gender, race, or even subject matter. Sometimes a single dominant personality can make every endeavor a challenge for the facilitator or derail entire meetings.

Although most of us would prefer smooth sailing, this interpersonal context is the reality for many PLCs. Another reality is the need to find a way to work with such dynamics. Changing what we do in the classroom is a breeze compared with addressing interpersonal baggage that, in some cases, existed long before the PLC was even formed. To illustrate this point, let's revisit the 8th grade social studies PLC that we've been observing in the Fly on the Wall vignettes. This PLC could be any PLC in any school in any state. At this point, we've got a pretty good handle on the members' roles and personalities:

- **Angie** is the hard-working, selfless facilitator of the team.
- **Bruce** is an openly disengaged and skeptical 15-year veteran.
- **Cassandra** is a skilled and popular but opinionated teacher.
- **Devin** is the compliant one, reluctant to make waves.
- **Evelyn** is the traditional but nurturing veteran on the team.

As facilitator, Angie has a lot on her plate. First, she needs to keep the dominant voices in check—including Cassandra, who is an ally to Angie and a valuable member of the team. Often, the teachers who dominate airtime are not aware that they are doing so, and they generally respond appropriately when it is brought to their attention. Angie also needs to bring Devin into the work more than she is currently doing: compliance without commitment can be a dangerous thing, although it is better than noncompliance. Evelyn, thorny at times, probably requires more validation and affirmation than the others do. She may see the profession she has loved all these years morphing into something unfamiliar and at a rate with which she is having difficulty keeping up. Angie would do well to reflect on ways in which she can capitalize on Evelyn's experience and her ties with the community at large. Bruce is probably Angie's biggest challenge. He has been around for a while, has seen initiatives come and go, and is perfectly complacent with being an OK teacher and a good coach. Might he be a good candidate for being helped by the PLC early in the process? Does he have work he's willing to share? If so, and if the meeting in which his work is shared goes well and is truly helpful to him, he may become much more interested in the PLC—maybe even an ambassador for it.

Having Bruce be the first member to bring his work to the PLC may seem counterintuitive; Cassandra probably seems like a stronger candidate. After all, she believes in the PLC, her ego can take it, and what happens with her can set a good precedent for other members who present their work in the future. That said, teachers like Bruce often volunteer to bring work first. They often have little invested in the work and are seemingly incapable of feeling judged by the team. These qualities actually make Bruce a good candidate: he'll surely be interested if *his* work is on the table, and he's teacher-tough enough to hear suggestions—which he will, his work being generally mediocre—and the whole team will benefit from the process. As Bruce's work improves, he will feel less skeptical of PLC work. Another benefit of having Bruce bring his work first is that because his work is of average quality, he is less threatening to his fellow team members; by contrast, the team may not relate as well to Cassandra's work. In this case, Cassandra might better serve the PLC as a fellow team member discussing a colleague's work. Her ideas, her ability to think below the surface, and her motivation to be of service to students will come across as helpful—as long as Angie knows when to rein her in so that she does not dominate the discussion.

The interpersonal complexities in facilitating this or any PLC are many. It would be nice if facilitators had only to worry about guiding a team through the steps of a protocol or leading data discussions. But the reality is that interpersonal context is all-important to a team's success. ***At the heart of it, PLCs are a human endeavor.***

The Nature of Change

Belonging to authentic PLCs makes a significant difference in teachers' practice, which in turn increases both the quality and quantity of student learning. Authentic PLCs compel teachers to explore how they are currently teaching, assessing student learning, and reacting when students don't learn, as well as to learn how to review and respond to data, engage in collaborative and reflective dialogue with one another, and use protocols to increase the focus, effectiveness, and fairness of professional conversations.

Belonging to an authentic PLC yields significant rewards for both teachers and students: teachers teach better. Students learn better. PLC members become part of an interdependent community that they have created. Most of all, being part of an authentic PLC is the first time many teachers truly feel like professionals. Teachers are often held in lesser regard by parents, students, and even themselves. When an authentic PLC wraps up an instruction-changing meeting of **substance with safety,** its members leave feeling like professionals. In my 25-plus years doing this work, I always leave such meetings feeling proud to be an educator and impressed by how professionally teachers comport themselves when they are operating in an environment that supports it.

But this can't happen unless we're daring enough to change our ways of thinking and our ways of meeting. Making this leap from business as usual to the unknown requires team members to place an enormous amount of trust in the process and the facilitator and to have the courage to say, "OK, I'll give this an honest try." That some teachers would be reluctant to plunge in is normal and should be expected. This degree of change requires risk taking—which is why it is essential to **build the team before you need it** and foster a culture of safety. Even when an authentic PLC and a culture that invites risk taking have been established, change is not easy.

To further illuminate our understanding of change, let's look at three relevant facts about human change that have emerged from the research (Evans, 2001; Fullan, 2016; Reeves, 2009; Stangor, 2011).

1. *Changing behavior precedes changing attitudes.* The converse may seem true—that we must change our attitudes to change our behavior—but that sequence applies more to self-initiated change than to extrinsically initiated change. For the latter, it is best to focus on changing people's behaviors. If all goes reasonably well, a change in attitude will follow. The saying "Fake it till you make it" comes to mind.

2. *People's acceptance of change is a function more of what the change means to them personally than of the actual merits of the change.* We can know intellectually that a change is good, either for us as teachers or for our students, and still resist it because of what it implies for us personally. For this reason, bombarding people with statistics or research showing why a change is a good idea is often ineffective. What's more effective is helping

people fit the change into their existing schemas so that the change makes sense on a personal level.

3. *People change when the pain of staying the same becomes greater than the pain of changing.* Henry Cloud made this insightful remark in *Boundaries: When to Say Yes, How to Say No to Take Control of Your Life* (Cloud & Townsend, 2012). Few precepts in the psychology of human change ring truer than this one when it comes to teachers' adaptation to the culture shift required by their membership in an authentic PLC. At some point, when the tipping point of cultural change is reached, teachers will find it more difficult to resist the change than to embrace it.

Reluctant and Resistant Teachers

Given humans' natural tendency to avoid change and the complex psychological adjustments required to embrace it, it is little wonder that school change agents are often met with some degree of opposition. But there is a difference between teachers who are *reluctant* to fully embrace the work of the PLC and teachers who are actively *resistant* to it.

Reluctant Teachers

In *The Practice of Authentic PLCs,* I explain the reluctant teacher:

> *Reluctant* teachers are quite commonplace, especially in the early days of forming a working PLC. In fact, I have never known a PLC in which at least one member was not reluctant or skeptical to embrace the work and climate of a true PLC. Reluctant teachers are typically questioning and disagreeing—even downright negative at times—but they tend not to be ill-intentioned. That is, they aren't negative for reasons that stem from self-serving motives; they simply aren't "buying it" yet and need time to see the merits of the work before they are willing to invest their time and energy. They are *reluctant,* and they are less likely than other members to roll up their sleeves and give the new ideas a try. *Their motivation for their reluctance is doubt.* (Venables, 2011, pp. 125–126)

Some teachers are reluctant to change their behavior for external reasons— say, for example, that their school has a history of constantly starting new initiatives and then abandoning them before they have had a chance to take root. This institutional memory is often the biggest impediment to giving the next good idea an earnest try—even if the good idea could really work. Other teachers are skeptical of change because they believe that colleagues will have difficulty implementing it or are unlikely to buy in to it. Their mindset is, "I would give this a try, but my coworkers won't, so why should I bother?" Still other teachers may feel skepticism about whether the change could work with *their* kids in *this* school. Time, of course, is always an issue for teachers; the fact that there is not enough of it makes teachers hesitant to embrace any change that may require a greater investment of it. There are other reasons why teachers feel reluctant to embrace proposed change, but these ring loudest in my experience.

It is the job of the skilled facilitator to listen to the concerns of reluctant teachers and to convince them with actions as well as words that the change will benefit them and their students. As discussed in Chapter 2, buy-in is not a binary concept; reluctant teachers will move closer to the buy-in end of the buy-in/buy-out continuum when they experience a critical mass of positive results stemming from the change. When facilitators do their jobs well—when they toe the line of authenticity without compromise and create a high-functioning PLC—every experience the PLC shares leaves team members feeling like accomplished, productive professionals. Every initially reluctant teacher has the potential to become an enthusiastic ambassador of PLC work. Ensuring that this happens is the facilitator's quest. Challenging? Of course—but the payoff is enormous.

Resistant Teachers and Saboteurs

Resistant teachers are a breed apart from reluctant teachers. Although they are fewer in number, they can present the biggest challenge a PLC facilitator has to face. In *The Practice of Authentic PLCs,* I explain:

> The demographics of resistant teachers are very often characterized by teachers who have been in the system for many years, teachers who have become jaded through the years by having been disappointed one too many times by failing initiatives in which they *did* personally invest, or teachers who are resentful of advancements that have worked in which they chose not to be a part. They may be resentful of a principal who is 20 years their junior. They may have extremely small and tightly defined comfort zones; anything happening outside those zones is viewed as a threat. . . . *Their motivation for resistance is personal.* (Venables, 2011, p. 127)

Ego is not necessarily the driving force behind resistant teachers' behavior; it is more often a sense of self-preservation. Knowing this, PLC facilitators should proceed slowly, taking these team members step-by-step through the process of changing their behavior. When a classroom teacher has a student whose behavior is difficult to manage, the teacher tries everything she knows to get the student to participate, to desist distracting others, to show respect, to be successful. In most cases, there is something in the teacher's bag of tricks that enables her to change the student's attitude and behavior so that the student can benefit. Although the "bag of tricks" used for facilitating adults may be different from the one used in the classroom, the process is similar. Usually, the facilitator is able to foster a change in the teacher's attitude and behavior. Resistant teachers need validation and affirmation, and, most important, they need to experience a sense of success for each change in behavior they make, however small. Their voices must be listened to, if not always agreed with, and naysaying must be met with exploration: *Why do you think that? What would you rather see happen? What steps can we take to overcome that obstacle?*

Resistant teachers may never come around to fully changing their own behavior. In some cases, getting them to the point of not sabotaging the rest of the team is a big victory. But if all battles with them are lost and their behavior impedes the work and growth of the rest of the team, then—just as the classroom teacher does with a persistently problematic student—the facilitator should bring the issue to the attention of the administration. The litmus test for when to do so entails asking questions such as *How much damage is this resistant teacher doing to the rest of the team? Is he or she negatively influencing the attitudes and behaviors of other PLC members? If unchecked, what is the natural progression of such behavior and influence on the team?* and *Do the growth and success of the team depend on this situation being changed?* If the answers to these questions indicate a need for intervention, the facilitator should feel no hesitation or guilt in seeking administrative support.

Compliance Versus Commitment

Sometimes, as is the case with resistant teachers, getting teachers to comply with what we're trying to do is a major accomplishment. But that's not the goal for the team. The goal is to have a team of teachers who are committed to engaging fully in the work of an authentic PLC in a way that produces a measurable effect on student learning.

Compliance is not altogether a bad thing, but it is not enough. In the early days of a PLC, before team members have experienced cogent meetings and long before they see results in their students' learning, it may be enough for them to merely comply with what facilitators are trying to do. If they trust the process, trust the facilitator, give it a try, and suspend skepticism long enough to experience the culture of an authentic PLC, compliance will likely turn into commitment. Once again, it is the facilitator's responsibility to ensure that each experience had by the PLC is productive and demonstrates to members the potential of the work. ***Make the meeting meaningful.***

Compliance can happen as soon as the PLC begins its work; commitment takes more time to develop. Once established, commitment is not easily reversed. PLC facilitators should not expect to rush the process but, rather, ***trust the process*** and keep plugging away at running productive meetings, knowing that attitudes will shift as the good work yields its rewards.

Bleeding Arteries

There are times in the life of an authentic PLC when an issue arises that must be addressed right then and there in order for the PLC to continue its work. These times are rare, but when they happen, the world of the PLC stands still until they are resolved. I call these *bleeding arteries*.

Most of the time, bleeding arteries have to do with the humanity of the team and may involve hurt feelings, flaring tempers, harsh words, or tears. But they do not always stem from interpersonal conflict. Sometimes a team member is going through personal circumstances that are unrelated to the PLC but affect the teacher so tempestuously that it becomes obvious to the team that something is deeply wrong. Although it is not the team's place to attempt to solve the problem or counsel the teacher, it may become apparent that ignoring the situation would show an uncaring, disrespectful attitude toward the team member's state of mind. We are humans first and PLC members second. With that in mind, I suggest four *T*s to help facilitators handle bleeding arteries:

- *Trash the agenda.* Scrap whatever you had planned for the meeting. This situation is too important. The future strength of your team will depend on what you do next, so it had better not be simply moving along to the next item on the agenda.
- *Transparency is crucial.* It is imperative for you and the rest of the team, with your encouragement, to be transparent about what is happening. The last thing you should do is pretend everything is fine. It's difficult to face the problem in an open way, but it is the only way to eventually move forward. Feeling awkward is a frequent occurrence when in the throes of a growth spurt.
- *Take time for the teacher to talk it out.* To the extent that she is willing, give the teacher the space and time to tell you and the team whatever she wishes to say about the situation. Gently prompting the teacher with questions can help break the ice. Remember that anything the teacher may say is for her benefit, not the team's. Above all, remind the team that everything discussed should be held in strict confidence.
- *Teacher's needs supersede the team's needs.* At this time, during this meeting, the needs of this teacher come before the needs of the rest of the team. Everything should be about this team member, not the facilitator or the rest

of the team. The team's responsibility is to rally around the teacher in need. The facilitator's responsibility is to ensure that this happens in a gentle and caring way.

The four *T*s approach can also be effective in the case of hard feelings between two teachers. Mediating such conflict is best done when the facilitator does more listening than talking and more asking than telling. The facilitator's role is not to take sides, even when she strongly favors one side or the other, but to solicit opinions from both parties and ask occasional follow-up questions for clarity. Radiating calm is crucial. When the facilitator stays calm, even during intense moments, it has a calming effect on the two teachers and the rest of the team.

Sometimes a bleeding artery occurs because a team member has demonstrated a significant misunderstanding of something important related to teaching and learning—for example, a math teacher whose only notion of differentiating lessons is to give the weaker students twice as many problems to complete. This kind of misunderstanding can have serious consequences for the teacher's students and implications for his or her influence over the rest of the PLC. In these instances, the misunderstanding needs to be addressed and cleared up so that the team and the teacher can move forward. It is important for the facilitator to do this in a tactful, uncondescending way. But letting it go and not speaking up is never the right plan of action.

Generally speaking, good things don't happen in a PLC when issues that need addressing are not addressed. Failing to deal with bleeding arteries will likely do immediate and long-term damage to the team. As unpleasant and awkward as it might be to face such situations, facilitators really have no choice if they want their teams to thrive. And coming out on the other side relatively unscathed makes the team stronger, with a newfound respect for the facilitator, the process, and one another permeating every meeting thereafter.

Summing Up

As we conclude Part 1 of this book, it should be apparent that facilitating a team of colleagues can be hard and complex work. Figure 4.1 lists the most common reasons for dysfunction within a PLC; although not all of these connect directly to interpersonal dynamics within the PLC, make no mistake: they all come down to *people*.

With practice, facilitators will internalize the essentials of facilitating colleagues, building trust and buy-in, and dealing with interpersonal obstacles, and these tasks will become second nature. In Part 2, we will keep in mind this human side of facilitation while taking a closer look at facilitating particular protocols and tasks common in the work of authentic PLCs.

FIGURE 4.1 | Common Reasons for Dysfunctional PLCs

A PLC may be dysfunctional because . . .

- It lacks administrative priority and leadership.
- The PLC is too big.
- The PLC facilitator is insufficiently trained.
- The school or the PLC has new leadership.
- It lacks faculty buy-in.
- It was poorly rolled out to staff.
- It is allotted little or no meeting time.
- The PLC process was rushed, with the team engaging in challenging or high-risk tasks before it has built a bedrock of trust and buy-in.
- The school has a history of failed initiatives.
- The PLC facilitator lacks commitment.
- The PLC has consistently yielded no improvement in student achievement.
- There is a prevailing lack of trust in the school's culture.
- The facilitator or administrators do not follow through on what they say they'll do.

Part 2:
Facilitating Tasks of Authentic PLCs

In Part 1, we discussed the whole gamut of aspects relating to facilitating teachers and teacher teams. In Part 2, we turn to specific tasks that authentic PLCs engage in—including text-based discussions, discussions around teacher and student work, discussions of data, discussions surrounding teacher dilemmas, and collaborative planning time—and discuss the nuances of facilitating them effectively. These chapters include protocols commonly used by authentic PLCs and offer suggestions and strategies to help facilitators improve the quality of teacher discussions and avoid common pitfalls.

5 | THREE POWER TOOLS FOR FACILITATING PLC DISCUSSIONS

Teachers who are members of an authentic PLC commit their energies and thoughts to whatever task the PLC happens to be engaged in. Facilitators, themselves full-fledged members of the PLC, likewise devote themselves to these tasks—but they have the added responsibility of guiding the PLC through the tasks and doing their utmost to ensure that everyone's experience is meaningful, productive, and safe. Facilitators must maintain a continual awareness of how members of the PLC are receiving, processing, and responding to the team's tasks. Wearing these two hats—that of facilitator and that of PLC member—is not easy, but when the PLC is having a really good meeting, everybody involved knows. Few things are as rewarding for the PLC facilitator.

In this chapter, we'll explore what I refer to as the three "power tools" that aid the facilitator in guiding the PLC's endeavors: protocols, frontloading, and debriefing.

Facilitator Power Tool #1: Protocols

In Part 1, we learned that protocols help ensure rich, focused, and safe conversations about teaching and learning. In addition to serving this important purpose, protocols make the facilitator's job easier. Because of the way they are structured, well-run protocols assuage the need for the facilitator to constantly keep the team on task or curb individual members from dominating airtime, for example, since the protocol itself requires these things. In this way, protocols are the facilitator's "best friend"—provided that they are followed with fidelity. Many years of field-testing and many meetings experienced by authentic PLCs have demonstrated that the way they are designed to be used is the way they work best. The following is a rundown of the benefits of using protocols in PLC work.

- **Protocols keep the PLC focused.** Staying focused is always an important goal, but it is particularly crucial for meetings in which time is short or pressed with other agenda items. When a team begins to get off task, it is the facilitator's job to refocus the group. That job is made considerably easier when the team is following a protocol. When a protocol is followed as written, it is very hard for the team's focus to stray from the work at hand.

- **Protocols maintain honesty and teacher safety.** Teachers' freedom to say what they're thinking about a team member's work and that team member's sense of safety are not mutually exclusive. In an authentic PLC, both cultural norms exist: teachers feel safe enough to share *and* hear honest contributions from one another because those contributions are made with great respect toward the receiving teacher and with the sole intention of helping his or her work improve. Safety and honesty are both essential elements in authentic PLCs, and they work in tandem. PLCs that are safe but not honest, or honest but not safe, are ineffective. It is interesting to note that the forebears of PLCs were called Critical Friends Group® (CFG) communities—*critical* in this context meaning crucial to success rather than implying criticism of other people or work. It was also common for CFG facilitators to point out to teachers that "critic" and "friend" were two necessary sides of the same coin: neither worked effectively without the other.

- **Protocols level the playing field.** When teachers engage in unbridled discourse, an inevitable imbalance in their contributions arises. Some teachers dominate the airtime and the consequential groupthink, others participate less forcefully but still freely, and still others may not speak at all. For some quiet teachers, this is just their personal style; they tend to process ideas internally rather than think aloud. But other times teachers are silent because they feel bulldozed by the dominant ones, and too often they withdraw from the discussion altogether. Worse, the vocal teachers are often completely unaware of the effect they are having on the quiet ones. Although a good facilitator notices this dynamic, it can be difficult to jump in and attempt to correct the problem. Protocols are effective at disabling this scenario. Their very structure requires all voices to be heard, and they often ask teachers to write down a response to a prompt quietly and individually before getting into the thick of the discussion. By giving everyone personal time to reflect on the prompt and then laying out a clear process for sharing, protocols level the playing field. Although the talkative teacher may still be the most vocal, the probability of him or her dominating the discussion and shutting down other teachers is appreciably lessened.

- **Protocols ensure efficient use of time.** I suspect 10 of 10 teachers would agree that they never have enough time to do all that they want or are asked to do. Time is a coveted commodity in schools. When followed with fidelity, protocols are intensely efficient in the use of time and lead to some of the most productive meetings teachers can have. Protocols enforce a respect for time that doesn't normally exist when teachers assemble to discuss teaching and learning. In the absence of protocols, discourse can quickly veer off topic and wind up in the we-didn't-accomplish-a-thing-at-this-meeting zone (WDAATATM, pronounced "we-dat-at-em"). This most dreaded type of meeting conveys a complete *disrespect* for (teachers') time. Once teachers become accustomed to using protocols and have experienced time-efficient, productive meetings, they develop a low tolerance for the time-wasting meetings of old. This is a signature earmark of a shifting faculty culture.

- **Protocols get results.** When an authentic PLC has finished a 45-minute meeting using a protocol to examine teacher work, the work improves—not only the work of the presenting teacher but also the work of *all* the teachers on the team. A casual observer of the meeting might see a half-dozen teachers keenly and uninterruptedly focused on improving one teacher's work. What would be invisible to that observer is the fact that all of the team members are, at various points throughout the protocol, thinking about *their* work, *their* assignments, *their* rubrics, *their* students. This is what catapults the experience beyond a simple review of teacher work, to leave a far-reaching, long-lasting imprint on the various kinds of work that any of the team members will produce thereafter.

- **Protocols make the facilitator's job easier.** Although it is personally and professionally rewarding, make no mistake: the facilitator's job is not an easy one. The goal is to guide a team of colleagues through experiences that enrich them as teachers and improve their instruction, and frankly, facilitators need all the help they can get. Without protocols, it is much more difficult to reel in a conversation that has gone adrift or focus on the work at hand instead of personal agenda items. Protocols make it easier for facilitators to guide their teams in doing this important work without undue strain, stress, or compromise.

Protocol Cautions

Despite the considerable benefits of using protocols, facilitators who are just starting to use them tend to make a few common mistakes. Consider the following four "caution statements."

- **Caution #1: Avoid merely going through the motions.** It is important to keep in mind that the goal is never *doing* the protocol. The goal is to have a structured, rich conversation around student or teacher work, or to set useful norms, or to assist a colleague in handling a dilemma she's facing in her class—you get the idea. The protocol is a tool for achieving the goal, not the goal itself. I have seen PLCs go through the motions of a protocol without having a conversation that actually results in better classroom instruction. When we think of a protocol not as the goal but as a tool for achieving a specific result, that specific result will likely be achieved.

- **Caution #2: Avoid falling victim to initial awkwardness or pushback.** Teachers unfamiliar with protocols are used to free-form discussions in which any tangentially related topic is fair game. Protocols don't allow this. Consequently, it is fairly common for teachers to experience (and vocalize) an initial awkwardness with using protocols. They may report that the protocols are too rigid, don't allow for change in conversational direction, or suppress free thinking. They may even suggest that having a discussion using a protocol is "unnatural." Ironically, the teachers who complain the loudest about having to use protocols tend to be the same teachers who disdain meetings that accomplish nothing of substance (WDAATATM). Given a little time, however, with protocol experiences guided by a caring and careful facilitator, these teachers usually realize that the protocols they initially pushed back against are the very tools that keep the team focused during meetings and accomplishing substantive gains. The takeaway here for facilitators is to *stay the course,* pushing through any temporary awkwardness and not giving in to pressure to not use a protocol for a given task. You *and* the team will be better for it in the long run.

- **Caution #3: Avoid being too militant.** This is a tough one. As facilitators, we don't want to increase initial awkwardness by being too strict in following the protocol. Some protocols—even some individual segments of protocols—require tight facilitation, whereas others can work fine with looser facilitation. The challenge is knowing when to tighten the ranks and when to ease off. As a general rule, the higher the risk of teacher vulnerability or defensiveness, the tighter the facilitation should be. For example, a protocol for looking at teacher or even student work holds considerable risk of vulnerability for the presenting teacher and should therefore be facilitated fairly tightly. By contrast, a norm-setting protocol generally involves a low level of risk, so facilitators have more latitude in allowing minor deviations from the prescribed steps. An exception to this general rule is protocols for text-based discussions: although there is little risk involved, these protocols should be tightly facilitated to prevent participants from straying from the text, as they are wont to do. When in doubt, err on the side of being a little too tight rather than a little too loose, especially for early experiences with the protocol. Like a classroom teacher at the start of the school year, we can always loosen up in time, but it is much more difficult to be loose at first and try to tighten the reins later.

Facilitation should also be loosened *only* for good reasons—because the protocol entails low risk, or a divergent conversation is going someplace important, for example—never because the facilitator wants to avoid the unpleasantness involved in reeling in an off-task group or calling out a team member who's not following the protocol. In the end, facilitators should trust their instincts and tighten or loosen up facilitation based on what's happening.

In addition to striking an appropriate balance between tight and loose facilitation, facilitators should be aware of their tone and manner as they facilitate. It is possible and advisable to tighten facilitation when it is called for while simultaneously retaining a pleasant, welcoming disposition.

- **Caution #4: Avoid choosing the wrong protocol.** One thing that can deal a damaging blow to the protocol experience for members of the PLC is to engage in a protocol that is mismatched to the work. There are hundreds of protocols just a click away (see http://www.NSRFharmony.org), and although many have similar structures, each has its own nuances that make it more or less suitable for a given task or goal. Although I generally recommend that PLCs initially cycle through the half-dozen or so most useful and applicable protocols (most of which are discussed in subsequent chapters), I encourage facilitators to try new ones after the team has gained experience in effectively using protocols. When selecting a new protocol, facilitators should be aware that some are not very good. If a protocol is shallow, on the cheesy side, or too affective, for example, the teachers on the team may be turned off. Facilitators need to read carefully any protocol they are thinking of trying for the first time. In schools that have them in place, coaches' PLC meetings provide a perfect opportunity to try out new protocols with fellow facilitators before using them with individual PLCs.

Facilitator Power Tool #2: Frontloading

Seasoned facilitators are skilled at frontloading what they're asking their PLCs to do. *Frontloading* refers to the introductory comments made by a facilitator just before engaging his or her PLC in a particular task. These comments include a statement of purpose, which provides a reason for pursuing the task, as well as an explanation of how the task connects to the previous and future work of the PLC. Teachers routinely frontload activities in the classroom with students; preparing a PLC to engage in a new task isn't that different. Proper frontloading forestalls logjamming comments from teachers like "Why are we doing this?" "What is the point of this?" and "What does this have to do with what we did last week?" Taking a few minutes to frontload the task and shed light on where the team is headed wards off unnecessary grief for the facilitator.

Frontloading also gives the facilitator a chance to dislodge potential obstacles in the work the team is about to embark on. For example, warning teachers who are about to experience their first protocol that it may feel strange at first to speak only during specific segments of the protocol rather than in the usual free-form fashion helps disarm any awkwardness participants might feel with the unfamiliar process. Likewise, leading the team in a short exercise on warm and cool feedback to front-load a protocol that specifically calls for those two types of feedback can help make the experience run more smoothly. Above all, frontloading is a form of transparency; teams do better when there are no surprises. Even saying, "I'm not sure how this is going to go; let's give it a try and see if we like it" encourages teachers to be in *trial* mode rather than *judgment* mode, increasing the odds that the protocol will go well.

Facilitator Power Tool #3: Debriefing

Most protocols end with a *debrief* consisting of a short discussion focused on the *process* of the team's experience, including what worked, what could be done better next time, how members felt during the experience, and possible modifications to the process (e.g., increasing or reducing time allotted for certain segments). Comments related to the *content* of the team's experience are discouraged during the debrief. Although the entire discussion might take only five minutes, when done well, the debrief can accelerate a PLC's growth considerably. As Joe McDonald, author of some of the most useful and widespread protocols, has said, "If you haven't got time to debrief, then you haven't got time to do the protocol" (personal communication, 1993). All PLCs stand to grow from the community knowledge developed during the protocol and its thoughtful debrief. This is especially true for new PLCs or for teams just beginning to use protocols.

John Dewey (1938/2015) said, "We don't learn from our experiences; we learn from reflecting on our experiences." Debriefs encourage reflection, an essential practice of authentic PLCs. Just as teachers reflect on a lesson they've delivered or on recent test results, PLCs reflect on the work they have done at the conclusion of a particular collaborative task. Debriefing hastens growth in the PLC; protocols and processes that may have felt awkward on the first go-round become more refined, efficient, and effective in improving classroom instruction and student learning. The debrief also allows reluctant team members to speak their minds about the tasks the

PLC has engaged in; it is the perfect forum for lodging concerns and constructive criticism. PLCs that make a regular habit of mindful debriefing stand to grow twice as fast as teams that never reflect on what they've done or where they're going.

The following are examples of questions that facilitators may ask during a debrief:

- How did it go? Did you like this protocol?
- What worked well?
- What could we do better next time?
- What might we change for next time? How would that make it better?
- Did we rush the protocol?
- Did we go deep enough?
- Did we stay on task?
- Will our students benefit from our having done this? How?
- Have we experienced a growth spurt from the last time we engaged in this task [or a similar experience]? In what area?
- How often should we engage in this protocol/task/discussion? What makes sense?

The following Fly on the Wall, which picks up from our 8th grade social studies PLC's experience in Chapter 1 (see p. 17), shows how Angie debriefs the team's very first time using a protocol.

 **FLY ON THE WALL** | **The Scene:** The First Day of Protocols (Part 2)

What Happened

Angie and her team have completed all segments of the Notice & Wonder Protocol for Data as prescribed. Before they adjourn the meeting, they debrief what they have just experienced together.

Angie: Let's take a couple of minutes and talk about the process we've just been through. Try to avoid discussing the data or any content and focus on the process[1]: What did we think of using the N&W Protocol for looking at data? Did it feel awkward or flat at times? Was it rich at times? When and why? What could we do

(continued)

better the next time we use this protocol? What did I do that helped or hindered the process? Are our students better off for us having done this? How? Why?[2] Evelyn, give us five minutes on the clock, starting now. What do you all think?

The team immediately begins discussing the experience, with Cassandra starting the group off.

Cassandra: I liked it. Everyone contributed and pretty much equally so. If it wasn't structured like this, I would be talking constantly because I'm a talker.

Bruce: I don't know, I don't get why we can't respond to each other's observations. Aren't we supposed to be having a conversation?[3]

Angie allows a moment of silence, waiting to hear if someone wants to tag on to Bruce's comment. No one does. Devin and Evelyn both look at Angie, as if awaiting her response. She eventually does respond, directing her comment to Bruce.[4]

Angie: Bruce, did you feel like we were having a conversation at any point in the protocol?

Bruce: Yeah, I guess when you asked questions during the Notice round—no, I mean the Wonder round.

Angie: And now? Are we having a conversation?

Bruce: Yeah.

Angie (directing her comment away from Bruce and to the group): Based on your experiences, what might have happened if we looked at the same data and discussed it freely, with no structure?

Evelyn: What always happens: we would get off the subject.

Cassandra: And one or two of us would dominate the whole discussion.

Devin: I probably wouldn't have said a thing.

Angie: Protocols take a bit of getting used to, but if we give them a chance, they can work to our advantage. Several of us at facilitator training felt the same way as Bruce when we first started using protocols. But we soon realized that the protocols kept us focused [gesturing to Evelyn] and encouraged everyone to participate instead of just a few [gesturing to Cassandra].[5] Part of the reason why we're having this debrief is so that we can do them better; so keep asking questions and bringing up points to help us do that.

What's Worth Noting

[1]Having just spent the previous 30 minutes discussing content, the team may find it challenging to switch gears and discuss only process. Emphasizing this focus at the onset of the debrief helps pave the way for an on-task discussion.

[2]Angie is asking good questions to push her team's discussion of the process. Rather than asking all of these questions at the same time, however, it would work better if she doled them out while facilitating the debrief. One reason for this is that when facilitators ask a long, unbroken stream of questions, the members of the PLC tend to focus on and discuss the last question they heard.

[3]This is a common concern of teachers who are first exposed to using protocols. The fact that Bruce felt comfortable enough to state this—especially after Cassandra's positive comment—shows a degree of functionality of the team as a whole.

[4]When facilitators hear a comment like Bruce's, they have a tendency to bristle in defensiveness. Angie, however, maintains her composure as she addresses Bruce's concern with respect and not dismissiveness.

[5]With one sincere comment, Angie has skillfully validated three members of her PLC.

It can be helpful to think of frontloading and debriefing as the bookends to whichever task or protocol the team is engaging in. Together, they provide a strong support to the protocol, ensuring that PLC members are on the same page when they begin the task and, afterward, have a common understanding of how they did, how the facilitator did, and what they might do to improve the experience next time. Frontloading helps make the task successful this time; debriefing helps make the task even better next time.

Separating the Work from the Person

If you were to observe an authentic PLC during a meeting to which a teacher has voluntarily brought a piece of his or her work for consideration, you might be impressed by the degree to which team members are able to focus on the work, as opposed to the teacher who created it. Although it takes time for this mindset of separating the work from the person to fully take hold in a PLC, it precipitates honest feedback and discussion.

To foster this mindset, during protocol segments that involve feedback, it is prudent for the facilitator to request that the presenting teacher physically slide his or her chair back from the group. Teachers offering feedback have a natural tendency to look at the teacher receiving the feedback and use words like "you," "your students," or "your lesson," which can cause the presenting teacher to receive the feedback defensively, however valid or well-intentioned it is. Think how differently the following might be heard by the presenting teacher: *your rubric* (no separation between the work and the person), *her rubric* (some separation), *the rubric* (full separation).

Physically separating the presenting teacher from the rest of the team drives team members to focus on the work and to talk to one another rather than to the presenting teacher; it also enables the presenting teacher to avoid eye contact and take notes on a laptop while the team members discuss her work. Again, the key is that the team discusses "her work," not "her." If the presenting teacher is mentioned at all in the context of the work, she is referred to in the third person. When all eyes are not on her, she can focus on what people are saying rather than on how her reactions to the feedback may appear to the team. The result is that honest feedback is both offered and received with greater comfort.

Comfort + respect + candor + safety = quality feedback. These important qualities can be achieved sooner than most new facilitators realize, and when they are, PLC members view meetings as extraordinarily productive and helpful. These meetings can—indeed, *must*—be so much more than writing SMART goals or planning what we're going to teach next Tuesday. ***There is learning in the balance.***

The power tools discussed in this chapter can be put to good use in facilitating specific protocols to accomplish specific tasks. In Chapter 6, we'll examine four popular protocols teacher teams can use in learning from text. In addition to exploring some of the nuances of these protocols, we'll discuss an important linchpin of PLC work: *constructing community knowledge.*

6 | FACILITATING TEXT-BASED DISCUSSIONS

Central to the notion of an authentic PLC is the act of *constructing community knowledge* (Venables, 2011). When teachers construct new knowledge together in real time, they not only become stronger as a team but also experience content in a shared way that pays dividends in future discussions.

To illustrate, suppose an elementary school faculty attended a 90-minute after-school workshop on differentiation. All the teachers, to varying degrees, might then reflect on and plan ways to use the differentiation strategies they had learned. The workshop had helped build each teacher's *individual* knowledge. Now suppose that, unlike the other grade-level teams, the 4th grade team of teachers met for 30 minutes the day after the workshop to discuss what they had taken away from the experience and reflect on how they might incorporate differentiation strategies into their instruction. By choosing to discuss what they had learned and how it might apply to their instruction, the 4th grade teachers upgraded their individual knowledge to a *collective* knowledge; that is, they constructed *community* knowledge. This act strengthened the team's professional practice as well as team members' relationships. But it did much more: by having developed a common understanding of what it means to apply differentiation strategies in the classroom, they gained a broader and deeper understanding of differentiation and became much more likely to implement the strategies (Venables, 2011). Moreover, in any future conversation that touches on differentiation, team members can call upon their shared understanding of this notion rather than the individual knowledge of differentiation strategies they garnered from simply attending the workshop. The power is in collective understanding and application. Figure 6.1 (see p. 74) lists tasks that help PLCs effectively build community knowledge.

Constructing Community Knowledge Through Text-Based Discussions

A highly effective way for a team to construct community knowledge is to engage in a text-based discussion. The first step is to select a text that addresses some aspect of teaching and learning that PLC members wish to learn more about or an area in which

FIGURE 6.1 | Tasks That Construct Community Knowledge

A PLC can build community knowledge by . . .

- Unpacking standards.
- Setting group norms.
- Debriefing any protocol or activity the team has undertaken.
- Reading and discussing a common text (e.g., an article or a book chapter).
- Scoring and discussing the same student work (calibrating).
- Scoring and discussing an instructional activity under consideration (e.g., using the Planning Protocol Rubric).
- Looking at and discussing teacher work.
- Looking at and discussing student data.
- Designing common assessments (including alternative assessments such as project-based learning assessments).
- Discussing instructional strategies for intervention.
- Setting and discussing SGOs (student growth objectives) and SLOs (student learning outcomes).

the data show gaps in learning or instruction. It's important for facilitators to keep in mind that authentic PLCs participate in text-based discussions not for the personal edification of their members, but because the knowledge gleaned from such discussions can influence what teachers do in the classroom. Because authentic PLCs may have as few as two text-based discussions in a school year—realistically, there isn't enough meeting time to have them very often—the text needs to be carefully selected by the team. The most meaningful text-based discussions occur when PLC members perceive a need to learn the content *and* have a say in choosing the text they'll be reading.

For example, the members of a 4th grade math PLC who want to align their instruction with the school goal of writing across the curriculum but who aren't sure how to incorporate writing in math may decide to read a text about writing in elementary math. Once the content is chosen, team members should have a voice in which specific text they will read. To this end, periodicals and other resources arranged around themes or topics (e.g., *Educational Leadership* magazine, *Kappan* magazine, or www.edutopia.org) are very useful. If a PLC is looking for content on, say, teaching students with disabilities, formative assessment, or reading in the content areas, the facilitator can pull up the table of contents of a pertinent periodical or the topic listing on a website to share with team members, who can then decide which article seems most salient or applicable to their needs. Buy-in is high when teachers choose the content and the text together; it's hard for teachers not to read the article when they themselves had a hand in picking it.

Once the text has been selected, the team members read it on their own, outside of the PLC meetings. The next time the team members convene, they discuss the text and its implications for their classroom instruction. The community knowledge constructed during these discussions gets all team members on the same page regarding the topic discussed and extends beyond the meeting room and into their classrooms. Further, this knowledge is completely organic, owned by the team rather than handed down from the administration.

The structure of text-based discussions generally follows a protocol. In the following sections, we will explore four popular protocols that can help facilitators lead productive text-based discussions: the Text-Based Seminar, the Four *As* Protocol, the Final Word Protocol, and the Essential Highlights Protocol.

Text-Based Seminar

More a set of guidelines than a detailed protocol, the Text-Based Seminar provides a framework for a team of teachers to discuss any text. The guidelines, laid out in Figure 6.2, come from the National School Reform Faculty.

Timing depends upon number of participants, complexity of text, and participants' time available. For a group of 15, this protocol can run between 20 and 50 minutes. Here are the segments I generally recommend for a 40-minute Text-Based Seminar:

1. Review of Text-Based Seminar guidelines and purpose. Share framing question, if applicable. (2 minutes)

FIGURE 6.2 | Text-Based Seminar Guidelines

Purpose: To enlarge understanding of a text (not achieve some particular understanding)

Ground Rules:

1. Listen actively.
2. Build on what others say.
3. Don't step on others' talk. Silences and pauses are OK.
4. Let the conversation flow as much as possible without raising hands or using a speaker's list.
5. Make the assumptions underlying your comments explicit to others.
6. Emphasize clarification, amplification, and implications of ideas.
7. Watch your own airtime—both in terms of how often you speak and in terms of how much you say when you speak.
8. Refer to the text; challenge others to go to the text.

Source: NSRF. Special permission has been received to reproduce the Text-Based Seminar from the National School Reform Faculty. See http://www.nsrfharmony.org or call 812-330-2702 for more resources and to learn about coaches' training to use NSRF resources most effectively.

---

2. Text-based discussion. (25 minutes)
3. Discussion of implications for practice. (8 minutes)
4. Debrief of the process. (5 minutes)

To effectively facilitate this seminar, it is helpful to keep in mind the following ground rules.

Emphasize that the sole purpose of the discussion is to understand the text. It is crucial that PLC members understand that the Text-Based Seminar is not meant to target specific learning or meet an intended outcome; its only goal is to increase the group's understanding of the text discussed. This is very different from the (entirely appropriate) learning goals that classroom teachers set for students who are reading an assigned text. The facilitator of a PLC is not a teacher in a classroom, and his or her job is to facilitate the discussion, not to lead team members to some predetermined knowledge or way of thinking. What team members get out of the text as a result of the discussion is exactly what they are supposed to get out of the text.

Refrain from autobiographical litanies. If there's one phrase that can single-handedly shut down a room full of teachers, it's "What *I* do is . . . ." Although it is appropriate in a Text-Based Seminar to share information about our own practice as it relates to the text, it is inappropriate and off-putting for a team member to go on at great length about what *he* does in the classroom. In short, select autobiographical comments are appropriate; monologues are not.

Make it a practice to ask follow-up questions. As the facilitator, you're there to guide the discussion as it develops organically. There will be times when a participant makes a point that you think should be explored further by the team. The best way to encourage such exploration is to ask a follow-up question of either the teacher who made the point or the team as a whole. For example, suppose during a protocol in which the team is discussing a blog post on homework policies, one member makes a comment suggesting that her sense of the purpose of homework is different from the others'. Seizing the moment, you say, "Jan's comment gets at the whole purpose of assigning students homework. Why *do* we give kids homework?" Note that you are affirming the contributing teacher, but not by sharing your own opinion; that would be *delivering* community knowledge. Rather, you are soliciting team members' opinions about the point raised and, in doing so, guiding them to *construct* community knowledge. In general, follow-up questions like "What do you all think about Tom's comment?" "Do you all agree?" or (to Tom) "Where in our practice do you find that to be true?" help push a team's thinking to a deeper level. Of course, the facilitator may ask a follow-up question based on the text rather than on a teacher's comment. However, when a follow-up question *is* based on a teacher's comment, it has the added bonus of validating a PLC member's contribution. ***Strengthen the team at every opportunity.***

Again, the point is not to impose our agendas as facilitators but, rather, to go deeper into the text and its implications for our instruction. Follow-up questions, even sparingly used, can be extremely beneficial in making the Text-Based Seminar the best experience possible for the PLC.

Challenge the team to stick to the text. The Text-Based Seminar usually calls for the facilitator to pose a framing question to guide the discussion. According to the NSRF protocol, it's important to

> Invest time in creating the framing question. It needs to be substantive, clear, relevant to the participants' experience, and likely to push their thinking in new directions. Above all, constructing a response to the question should require close reading of the text. We recommend that the framing question be genuine for everyone, including the facilitator, so that the entire group is engaged in the inquiry. Framing questions are often based on a quote from the text, which begins to establish a pattern of using the document as a basis for the conversation. (para. 5)

Be certain that your framing question does not undermine the purpose of the seminar; framing questions should never try to elicit some particular understanding of the text. Although framing questions are designed to help focus the team and deepen the conversation, they are often poorly written and achieve the opposite. If a framing question is too imposing or itself reflects shallow thinking, the seminar discussion can be limited rather than fortified by the question. For this reason, I suggest that facilitators who are comfortable crafting careful framing questions do so and those who are not avoid them altogether. A word of warning: in the absence of a framing question, the facilitator may need to facilitate the discussion more tightly to keep participants focused on the text.

Discuss implications for practice. Engaging in a text-based discussion is in itself a worthwhile endeavor for a PLC: the team becomes stronger, more cohesive, and more knowledgeable just by having experienced the process. The community knowledge constructed will inform future discussions and decisions related to the text's content. That said, we as facilitators would be remiss if we did not engage our teams in a discussion about the implications of the text for our practice. Indeed, some team members will see little value in the text-based discussion unless it also addresses next steps or changes teachers can make in the classroom. This is why I add an 8-minute segment of the Text-Based Seminar specifically encouraging the team to discuss implications of the text for their practice. For example, after a PLC read—at my suggestion, an article on giving students feedback on written assignments (Chappuis, 2012)—the team members became aware of the notion of "differentiated feedback" and routinely implemented it thereafter on every written assignment they gave. They quite likely would never have made this change to their practice had they not read the text and discussed its implications.

Four *As* Protocol

In contrast to the Text-Based Seminar, which can be quite fluid and organic, the Four *As* Protocol is a bit more scripted, consisting of rounds. Each round is driven by a prompt asking participants to name a different *A* from the text. The rounds, in order, consist of the following:

Round 1:   What do you ***agree*** with in the text?
Round 2:   What ***assumptions*** does the author make?
Round 3:   What do you want to ***argue*** with in the text?
Round 4:   What part(s) of the text do you ***aspire*** to (or wish to ***act*** on)?

This order is what I have found works best with teachers, although it deviates slightly from the original NSRF protocol (2005). As the team progresses through the rounds, each teacher shares his or her answer to the prompts.

The Four *As* Protocol is easier to facilitate than the Text-Based Seminar because of its structure. Also, team members have equal voice as they share their *As* in turn; unlike the Text-Based Seminar, it is nearly impossible for one team member to dominate the conversation. In fact, there is little conversation, if any. Facilitators, as always, may interject follow-up questions to encourage some brief discussion on important points raised by the team, but aside from this, little discussion happens. This makes the Four *As* Protocol a good choice for a text-based discussion that needs to happen in a limited time frame.

Another appealing attribute of the Four *As* Protocol is that it gives teachers—particularly crabby teachers—a built-in forum to disagree with the author of the text. This encourages reluctant teachers to participate. In the end, what they disagree with doesn't matter as much as the opportunity to have their voices heard in a structured way.

As with the Text-Based Seminar, I like to include a segment for PLC members to discuss implications for practice. The times for a 35-minute Four *As* Protocol follow:

1. Individual review of text, annotations, highlights. Teachers write down their 4 *As*. (7 minutes)
2. Rounds 1–4. (15 minutes)
3. Discussion of implications for practice. (8 minutes)
4. Debrief of the process. (5 minutes)

Final Word Protocol

Like the Four *As* Protocol, the Final Word Protocol happens in rounds. The purpose of this protocol is to expand the team's understanding of a text in a focused way in a controlled amount of time. Figure 6.3 includes my adaptation of the original version by NSRF. It requires 55 minutes.

The nice thing about the Final Word Protocol is its structure. As long as facilitators adhere to the rounds as prescribed, the team will stay focused on the text and all voices will be equitably heard. Some team members may initially push back at the rigidity of the rounds determining who speaks when, but in the end, participants usually realize how helpful the protocol was in focusing the team and ensuring its efficient use of time. If teachers still find the protocol too rigid, they may voice that concern during step III, when the team debriefs the process.

FIGURE 6.3 | Final Word Protocol

Time: 55 minutes

I. Team members individually highlight or annotate the common text that they have already read. Each person selects one or two significant quotes or sections from the text. Each excerpt should consist of at least a sentence but be no longer than a short paragraph. (6 minutes)

II. Participants work in groups of four,* with a designated timekeeper, facilitator, and first speaker for each round. The facilitator's role is to ensure that the group stays focused, while the timekeeper's role is to make sure that participants stick to the times. There are four rounds of 11 minutes each (44 minutes total). Here's what each round looks like:

1. The first speaker reads one of his or her selections from the text and then explains the significance of the excerpt and why he or she chose it. *Others in the group are not permitted to speak during this time.* (3 minutes)
2. Each participant, in turn, gets 2 minutes to comment on the first speaker's selection. Team members may choose to respond to what the first speaker has said *or* to speak to the excerpt itself in any way that extends the group's understanding of the text. No one is permitted to speak except the person whose turn it is to speak. (6 minutes)
3. After his or her fellow team members have spoken, the first speaker has the **FINAL WORD**. (2 minutes)

    Rounds 2, 3, and 4 begin by rotating the roles of first speaker, facilitator, and timekeeper.

III. The team debriefs the process. (5 minutes)

*Groups of five or six are also appropriate, although their rounds would require 65 and 90 minutes, respectively. Each round can be trimmed, if necessary. Divide a team with seven members into two groups, one of three and one of four, with the recognition that the larger group will finish after the smaller group. If time is limited, a team of six can also be split into two groups of three.

Source: NSRF. Special permission has been received to reproduce the Final Word Protocol from the National School Reform Faculty. See http://www.nsrfharmony.org or call 812-330-2702 for more resources and to learn about coaches' training to use NSRF resources most effectively.

Essential Highlights Protocol

The Essential Highlights Protocol is inspired by the Text Rendering Protocol, which was written by educators associated with the National School Reform Faculty (NSRF). In developing this protocol, I added the use of highlighters, which makes the rounds more visual and, I believe, more resounding in their effects. The purpose and rounds are outlined in Figure 6.4. This protocol requires 30 minutes.

The Essential Highlights Protocol works on several levels. First, as with most protocols, when it's well facilitated, the team stays focused and shares airtime equitably. It is very difficult for the team to get off topic or for one or two teachers to dominate the conversation.

Second, because teachers share pink-highlighted phrases that they themselves did not highlight, there is a degree of anonymity and safety in the sharing. This step

FIGURE 6.4 | Essential Highlights Protocol

Time: 30 minutes

Purpose: To collaboratively construct meaning from, clarify, and expand thinking about a text

Materials: Hard copies of the text to be discussed and highlighters in yellow, blue, and pink

Setup: Participants sit in a circle or around a conference table.

Roles: Facilitator, timekeeper

I. *Round 1:* Team members individually read and highlight the text as they normally would, using the *yellow* highlighter. Each then passes his or her highlighted copy of the text to his or her left-hand neighbor. (5 minutes)

II. *Round 2:* Team members individually read the highlighted portions of the text they have received from their neighbor and highlight in *blue* a single yellow-highlighted sentence from each yellow-highlighted excerpt in the text. No new sentences may be highlighted—only those previously highlighted in *yellow.* Each team member then passes his or her double-highlighted copy of the text to his or her left-hand neighbor. (5 minutes)

III. *Round 3:* Team members individually read the highlighted portions of the text they have received and highlight in *pink* a single phrase from each highlighted excerpt in the text. No new phrases may be highlighted—only those previously highlighted in *yellow* or in *yellow and blue.* Each team member then returns the text to its original owner. (5 minutes)

IV. Team members take turns sharing with the group the *pink*-highlighted phrases from their original copies of the text. (5 minutes)

V. The team discusses any new insights about the text that may have emerged. (5 minutes)

VI. The team debriefs the process. (5 minutes)

also disables any temptation team members may have to elaborate on their own selections. Facilitators may find this a useful strategy in other protocols or discussions, too: having participants share a different team member's comment or selection gives them no chance to elaborate, thus helping to ensure that the team stays focused and moves efficiently through the protocol. In addition, teachers tend to feel validated when a colleague takes seriously and shares their contributions, especially when it's done anonymously.

Finally, the Essential Highlights Protocol forces a distillation of the text to its fewest and most elemental points, and in an organic way; there is no way to steer participants or predict which parts of the text will end up pink. The activity is an exercise in constructing community knowledge in its purest form.

The Rewards of Text-Based Protocols

In the absence of a protocol, a text-based discussion is simply a free-form conversation that lacks structure and focus and, as a result, yields no clear learning, conclusions, or next steps. As teachers themselves will attest, when they meet, discussions can quickly stray from the meeting's agenda and focus until, 45 minutes later, they realize that little or nothing was accomplished.

Text-based protocols may seem a bit rigid at first, but the benefits of having a timely, focused, equitable discussion about important matters that affect teachers' instruction and students' learning outweigh any initial strangeness or discomfort teachers may feel. As I mentioned in Chapter 5, the teachers who express the greatest displeasure about protocols' structure tend to be those who complain the loudest when meetings have accomplished nothing of substance. Facilitators are well advised to tap into teachers' disdain for the latter to help justify the former.

In Chapter 7 we will delve deeply into facilitating the most powerful kinds of conversations PLCs can have: those surrounding student and teacher work. These are like the scariest yet most exhilarating ride at the amusement park. Armed with knowledge and protocols for facilitation, these discussions don't need to be a bumpy ride. Get ready for the excitement and the rewards in what follows—and keep your hands in the cart.

7 | FACILITATING DISCUSSIONS SURROUNDING STUDENT AND TEACHER WORK

More than once, I have stressed the importance of **building the team before you need it.** By the time your PLC begins discussing student and teacher work, believe me: you'll need it. Looking at student and teacher work is the most difficult and sensitive task teams can undertake, and arguably the most important. This is where we take an honest look at our effectiveness as teachers and engage in important conversations about improving our instruction. This is where the hard work of building a trusting, collaborative team pays off.

Meetings in which we carefully examine the work we do and the work our students produce as a result of what we do leave us feeling that we have truly made a difference. These are among the most professional and productive meetings PLCs can have. Writing SMART goals and planning the next unit's assessment pale in comparison to holding safe, honest conversations surrounding student and teacher work. In this chapter we will discuss several aspects of facilitating these delicate and rewarding discussions and explore two important protocols: the Notice and Wonder Protocol and the Tuning Protocol.

Why We Look at Student Work and Teacher Work

Looking at student work and looking at teacher work both serve the common purpose of providing us with information that we can use to improve our instruction. In the following sections, I dig more deeply into the hows and whys of each focus.

Looking at Student Work

It's important for PLCs to look at student work. After all, what students produce—good or bad—is evidence of how effective our instruction was. Student work is a mirror that reflects our work, and if we want to improve our craft, we need to sample the fruit of our labor.

As I can attest from personal experience, this process can be challenging. Sometimes we scratch our heads and wonder where students have been while we were teaching. But other times, their work exceeds our expectations. At times like these, we beam with pride and can't wait to show the work to our colleagues, and we wish that our spouses were in education so that they might fully share in our delight. No matter which scenario is at play, all of the teachers in a PLC learn a great deal from carefully reviewing student work, even when the work doesn't come from one of their own students.

Sometimes PLCs look at student work to calibrate their scoring. For example, suppose each member of a 9th grade English language arts PLC brings to a meeting two samples of narrative essays from a common assignment. The team members can individually score each essay against a scoring rubric and then discuss (and perhaps dispute) the scores together. A good way to construct community knowledge, this kind of exercise helps teachers calibrate not only their scoring of the work but also their definition of each dimension of the rubric (e.g., organization, creativity, descriptiveness). The team can use this shared understanding as a reference point going forward, well past the shelf life of the assignment discussed.

Looking at Teacher Work

Looking at student work is a vital endeavor of any serious PLC, but looking at teacher work arguably has an even greater impact. The reason is simple: student work happens after instruction has occurred, so any response teachers make based on looking at the student work is *reactive*. By contrast, teacher work—particularly work not yet implemented—happens before student work is produced, so changes or improvements made to it before implementation are *proactive*. For this reason, I suggest that PLCs look at teacher work two times for every one time they look at student work.

Looking at and discussing teacher work is both the most important exercise authentic PLCs engage in and the riskiest thing teachers can do in the PLC. On both counts, the PLC must proceed carefully so that these are the best, most consequential meetings the team has. The cycle of making ourselves vulnerable by putting our work out there and then benefiting from the conversation our colleagues have surrounding that work is the nexus of what it means to be in an authentic PLC. The net result is that everyone's work improves—and students reap the benefits.

But it's not easy. It requires careful facilitation, and I use *careful* here to mean "full of care." It takes a willingness to be vulnerable, a willingness to offer feedback—even when that feedback is constructively cool or points out gaps in the work—and a willingness to hear feedback with an open and objective mind, despite the very personal nature of teacher work. All of these things require a bedrock of trust among members of the PLC.

It is essential that this delicate work go well; teacher teams that experience anything but a supportive conversation focused solely on improving the work are unlikely to soon engage in one again. That would be to the detriment of the students. The following guidelines can help PLCs ensure that the experience of looking at a colleague's work is as effective and safe as possible:

1. The purpose of looking at teacher work is to help make the work better, not to *evaluate* or *critique* the work. Those terms, along with *constructive criticism,* have no place in this process. ***Elevate, don't evaluate (the work).***

2. The purpose of bringing work to be looked at is to help make the work better, because it is not as good as it could be and would benefit from discussion and suggestions from the team.

3. Because readiness to put forth one's work to be reviewed and discussed varies from team member to team member, the process requires that presenting teachers *volunteer* to bring work to be looked at; they are not coaxed into "taking a turn."

4. Teachers never bring their best work.

5. Facilitators stick closely to the protocol being used to examine the work.

6. Facilitators *only* facilitate; timekeeping and note taking are left to volunteers.

7. Facilitators ask follow-up questions of both individual teachers and the group, such as "Why do you see that as a gap?" "What do others think about that feedback?" or "What might Ms. Smith do to lessen that effect?" (For more ideas, see Figure 3.1, p. 40.)

8. Facilitators keep a keen eye on body language and other nonverbal cues, particularly those of the presenting teacher.

9. Job 1 of the facilitator is to maintain the safety of the presenting teacher. Job 2 is to push the discussion to as deep a level as possible while still doing Job 1.

10. Never omit or rush the debrief, which is where team growth spurts often happen. (For guidance on leading an effective debrief, see "The Mindful Debrief" [Venables, 2015b] in the Appendix, p. 153.)

11. A good ratio for the proportion of *warm feedback* to *cool feedback* to *suggestions* (see discussion on p. 92) is roughly 1:2:3. Our work will not improve very quickly if all we do is affirm the good parts and point out the gaps; suggestions are the fuel for the flame of improvement.

The usefulness of looking at teacher work depends on it being presented and reviewed in the spirit of improving the work. If the first two items on the preceding list are followed consistently, they quickly become a cultural touchstone of the PLC. When this culture of improvement is firmly entrenched, teachers realize that bringing their best work would defeat the purpose of the discussion: the whole point is to help turn decent teacher work into outstanding teacher work. But to create a culture where teachers feel comfortable enough to do this, facilitators need to remember the all-important Job 1 and Job 2.

The Notice and Wonder Protocol

I wrote the Notice and Wonder Protocol for looking at data in 2007. In the decade since, the Notice and Wonder Protocol has proven to be one of the most effective, versatile, and accessible protocols used by teacher teams: after all, anyone can notice, and anyone can wonder; teachers have remarkable ease and willingness doing both.

In this chapter, I discuss the Notice and Wonder Protocols for looking at student work and teacher work; in Chapter 8, I will discuss the Notice and Wonder Protocol for looking at data. All three versions have slight differences, but all of them consist of two rounds: in the first round, participants make Notice Statements, or nonevaluative, noninferential, objective statements about the work or data; in the second round, participants share Wonder Statements, which may be speculative, suggestive, challenging, or questioning.

One of the appealing features of the Notice and Wonder Protocol is that it manages to be safe and substantive at the same time. If Notice Statements are properly phrased, stating only what is objectively true, then there is little room to disagree with or challenge them, so presenting teachers should have no difficulty hearing them. It is only when teams allow inferences or evaluative language to slip into the Notice round that the safety and unassailability of the statements get jeopardized. That's a recipe for potential defensiveness on the part of the presenting teacher. Even the Wonder Statements, while containing elements of evaluation and sometimes skepticism, are couched as queries rather than hard-and-fast opinions. This format insulates the presenting teacher while preserving the integrity of the comments. Figure 7.1 (see p. 86) offers an overview of what Notice and Wonder Statements look like.

It is instructive to think of Notice Statements as *fact-finding* statements that draw our attention to what is already there; this initial round compels the team to think about the work in objective terms. By contrast, Wonder Statements can be thought of as *possibility-finding* statements that raise questions and draw our attention to what could be. In the Wonder round, concrete thinking gives way to the more powerful "what if" kinds of higher-order thinking that help the work get better—in an entirely nonthreatening, productive manner, if the protocol is followed as prescribed. The practice of looking at teacher or student work and thinking about ways to improve it rather than ways to criticize it helps build what Carol Dweck (2006)

FIGURE 7.1 | Notice and Wonder Statements at a Glance

	Notice Statements	Wonder Statements
What They Are	• Factual observations • Free of speculation, evaluation, and inference • Example: "I notice that/ how . . . ."	• Speculative, inferential, questioning, or challenging statements • Example: "I wonder why/how/ whether/if . . . ."
Facilitation Notes	• Remind participants to notice what is *present* in the work, not what is missing.	• Ask follow-up questions after select Wonder Statements (either of the wonderer or of the group as a whole). • Keep discussions resulting from follow-up questions brief. • Wonder Statements need not stem from previous Notice Statements.

and others refer to as a *growth mindset*—the belief that intelligence, rather than being fixed, can be developed.

To be sure, not all Wonder Statements are created equal; some contribute more to student or teacher growth than others. I find it helpful to delineate four levels of Wonder Statements:

- Lowest level: Wonder Statements about individual students
- Second-lowest level: Wonder Statements about the assignment (or assessment)
- Second-highest level: Wonder Statements about instruction that *has* happened
- Highest level: Wonder Statements about instruction that *could* happen

All Wonder Statements push the team's thinking to a higher level, but the real power lies in those that relate to instruction: reflections on what has happened and ideas about what could happen.

For a protocol consisting of two simple and safe activities—noticing and wondering—it can yield a surprising amount of growth in the PLC's work, in the presenting teacher's practice, and in the thinking of all the team members. It is no *wonder* that I've *noticed* teachers really like this protocol (puns intended). In the following sections, we'll explore using the Notice and Wonder Protocol for looking at student work and teacher work.

The Notice and Wonder Protocol for Student Work

The Notice and Wonder Protocol for student work requires 40 minutes; the steps are outlined in Figure 7.2 (see p. 88). As is the case with all protocols for looking at student and teacher work, there is a segment in which the presenting teacher reflects on what he or she has heard.

Again, it's important to ensure that Notice Statements are *fact-finding* statements. For example, a member of a Grade 3 PLC looking at samples of student solutions to a word problem might say, "I notice student *A* used two sentences to explain his approach." This Notice Statement is a factual observation based on what is already present in the work; it makes no attempt to draw a conclusion or make an implication. An example of an unacceptable Notice Statement would be "I notice student *A* was able to explain his work." This statement makes an inference or speculation about the student's *ability* when the observer doesn't actually know what he was capable of; the PLC members could see only what he *did*. This distinction might sound picky, but it bears repeating: when we allow inferences to stand during the Notice round, we veer from a relatively risk-free zone into one of vulnerability. Inferences are best left to the Wonder round, where a team member might say, "I wonder whether student *B* understands the solution or has simply memorized the steps."

The Notice, Like, and Wonder Protocol for Teacher Work

Given the delicate nature of looking at teacher work, it is imperative that a PLC's first few experiences using protocols to seriously examine teacher work go well. It is important to err on the side of safety rather than rigor during this early stage—and I know of no safer or more effective protocol for looking at a colleague's work than the Notice, Like, and Wonder Protocol. Figure 7.3 (see p. 89) provides an overview.

Despite providing a high level of safety for the presenting teacher, this protocol invites substantive contributions by the team. It is appropriate and encouraged to pose challenging or skeptical queries along with suggestions; after all, the presenting teachers bring their work to the team because they know it can be better. The goal of the PLC is to help improve this work while the facilitator focuses on his or her goal of balancing safety with substance.

The Notice, Like, and Wonder Protocol operates in essentially the same way as the Notice and Wonder Protocol. The most notable difference is the addition of a round in which participants offer Like Statements. These statements occur between the Notice and Wonder rounds and are deliberately evaluative insofar as

FIGURE 7.2 | Notice and Wonder Protocol for Student Work

Time: 40 minutes

Roles: Facilitator, timekeeper, presenting teacher

Purpose: To analyze student work

I. *The context.* (5 minutes)

- The presenting teacher gives the context for the work he or she has volunteered to share. Other team members are silent and take notes. (2 minutes)
- The presenting teacher distributes relevant documents for the team to review. (3 minutes)

II. *Clarifying questions.* The team asks clarifying questions of the presenter. These questions should be free of judgment; their sole aim is to elicit additional information. Answers to these questions are short, often a single statement. (5 minutes)

III. Quietly and individually, participants write three or four Notice Statements based on their observations of the work. These statements, which begin with the phrase "I notice that . . . ," must be free of inference, judgment, or speculation; they are fact-based, observing only what is already present in the work. (3 minutes)

IV. *Round 1: Notice Statements.* Team members take turns reading aloud one new Notice Statement at a time, *without discussion,* while the presenting teacher quietly takes notes. The process continues until all Notice Statements have been shared. (4 minutes)

V. Quietly and individually, participants write three or four Wonder Statements about the work. These statements, which begin with the phrase "I wonder why/if/how/whether . . . ," may or may not relate directly to Notice Statements shared in Round 1. Sometimes they offer a suggestion; other times they are merely inquiries to help the presenting teacher think more expansively about his or her work. (5 minutes)

VI. *Round 2: Wonder Statements.* In no particular order, team members take turns reading aloud one new Wonder Statement at a time while the presenting teacher quietly takes notes. This process continues until all Wonder Statements have been shared, *without discussion, except* in cases where the facilitator chooses to ask follow-up questions of a teacher sharing a Wonder Statement or of the whole team. (8 minutes)

VII. *Teacher reflection.* The presenting teacher takes a moment to review his or her notes and then reflects aloud on any or all of the comments made by the team. The rest of the team is silent. (5 minutes)

VIII. *The debrief.* The team members debrief the experience they have just shared. (5 minutes)

Source: The Notice and Wonder Protocol for Student Work (v2.0) is a protocol for looking at student work developed by Daniel R. Venables. From D. Venables, *The Practice of Authentic PLCs: A Guide to Effective Teacher Teams,* Corwin, 2011. Copyright 2011 by Corwin. Adapted with permission.

FIGURE 7.3 | Notice, Like, and Wonder Protocol for Teacher Work

Time: 50 minutes

Roles: Facilitator, timekeeper, presenting teacher

Purpose: Improving a teacher's (or teachers') work

I. *The context.* (5 minutes)

- The presenting teacher gives the context for the work he or she has volunteered to share. Other team members are silent and take notes. (2 minutes)
- The presenting teacher distributes relevant documents for the team to review. (3 minutes)

II. *Clarifying questions.* The team asks clarifying questions of the presenter. These questions should be free of judgment; their sole aim is to elicit additional information. Answers to these questions are short, often a single statement. (5 minutes)

III. Quietly and individually, participants write three or four Notice Statements based on their observations of the work. These statements, which begin with the phrase "I notice that . . . ," must be free of inference, judgment, or speculation; they are fact-based, observing only what is already present in the work. (3 minutes)

IV. *Round 1: Notice Statements.* Team members take turns reading aloud one new Notice Statement at a time, *without discussion,* while the presenting teacher quietly takes notes. The process continues until all Notice Statements have been shared. (4 minutes)

V. Quietly and individually, participants write three or four Like Statements based on their observations of the work. These statements, which begin with the phrase "I like . . . ," are based on personal preferences. (3 minutes)

VI. *Round 2: Like Statements.* Team members take turns reading aloud one new Like Statement at a time, *without discussion,* while the presenting teacher quietly takes notes. The process continues until all Like Statements have been shared. (5 minutes)

VII. Quietly and individually, participants write three or four Wonder Statements about the work. These statements, which begin with the phrase "I wonder why/if/how/whether . . . ," may or may not relate directly to Notice Statements shared in Round 1. Sometimes they offer a suggestion; other times they are merely inquiries to help the presenting teacher think more expansively about his or her work. (5 minutes)

VIII. *Round 3: Wonder Statements.* In no particular order, team members take turns reading aloud one new Wonder Statement at a time while the presenting teacher quietly takes notes. This process continues until all Wonder Statements have been shared, *without discussion, except* in cases where the facilitator chooses to ask follow-up questions of a teacher sharing a Wonder Statement or of the whole team. (10 minutes)

IX. *Teacher reflection.* The presenting teacher takes a moment to review his or her notes and then reflects aloud on any or all of the comments made by the team. The rest of the team is silent. (5 minutes)

X. *The debrief.* The team members debrief the experience they have just shared. (5 minutes)

Source: The Notice, Like, and Wonder Protocol for Teacher Work is a protocol for looking at teacher work developed by Daniel R. Venables. From D. Venables, *The Practice of Authentic PLCs: A Guide to Effective Teacher Teams,* Corwin, 2011. Copyright 2011 by Corwin. Adapted with permission. This version includes contributions from the fine folks at Caldwell-West Caldwell Schools.

they communicate attributes of the teacher work that the participants like. Like Statements provide an affirming bridge between the objective Notice Statements and the questioning Wonder Statements. Some examples of Like Statements include the following:

- I like how the dimensions of the rubric are weighted by importance.
- I like the degree of choice students have in this assignment.
- I like how many opportunities this lesson offers for students to use technology.
- I like that this really assesses understanding of the concepts and not simply procedural knowledge.

Because of the specificity of the Like Statements, the presenting teacher receives targeted information about what his or her teammates thought were high points of the work.

It is worth noting that the Notice, Like, and Wonder Protocol works fine without the Like round—which is the way I originally wrote it for teacher work. Some teams choose to include it, while others prefer to omit it. Either way, the protocol is incredibly effective for looking at teacher work and is a favorite of many teachers I've worked with throughout the United States.

The Tuning Protocol

The Tuning Protocol is perhaps the oldest, most extensively field-tested, and most widely used protocol out there for looking at student and teacher work. It is the grandfather of most, if not all, protocols used in education today. I was fortunate to learn the Tuning Protocol from its primary author, Joseph McDonald, back when he was a senior researcher for the Coalition of Essential Schools in the early 1990s. (A variation of McDonald's Tuning Protocol has been listed on the NSRF website since 1994. It has been updated after more than 20 years of experience across many settings, tying in current understanding of mindset and brain theory.) Although it was originally written for looking at student work, I believe it is best suited for looking at teacher work.

The version of the Tuning Protocol shown in Figure 7.4 is one I modified from McDonald's Tuning Protocol. It is a bit more streamlined than the 60-minute original version, requiring only 40 minutes; in my experience, PLCs rarely have a full hour to meet, so I try to design protocols (and modify existing protocols) to be less than 60 minutes in length. In particular, readers familiar with the original Tuning Protocol will notice that my shortened version does not include the focusing question, which the presenting teacher traditionally asks at the end of the first segment. The purpose of the focusing question is to direct feedback to a particular aspect of the work, as decided by the presenting teacher. A focusing question honors what is important to

FIGURE 7.4 | Tuning Protocol for Looking at Teacher Work

Time: 40 minutes

Roles: Facilitator, timekeeper, presenting teacher(s)

Purpose: Improving a teacher's (or teachers') work

I. *Presentation of work.* (5 minutes)

- The presenting teacher discusses the context for the work he or she has volunteered to share, including goals (teacher and student), whether he or she has already used the work with students or is planning to use the work, relevant information about the students or topic, and an area of focus for the feedback, if there is one. Other team members are silent and take notes. (3 minutes)
- The presenting teacher distributes handouts or supporting documents for the team to review. (2 minutes)

II. *Clarifying questions.* As participants review the handouts, they may ask clarifying questions of the presenter. These questions are fact-based (e.g., who, what, when, how long) and should be nonevaluative; their sole aim is to elicit additional information. The presenting teacher answers these questions in brief statements. (5 minutes)

III. *Participant reflection.* Participants continue to review the work and collect their thoughts about feedback they will share in segment IV. There is no discussion during this time. (5 minutes)

IV. *Feedback.* Participants talk with one another about the work, referring to the presenting teacher in the third person (if at all), while the presenting teacher quietly takes notes. The group begins with *warm* feedback (3–5 minutes) and then moves on to *cool* feedback, which may or may not be accompanied by suggestions (10 minutes). The facilitator may ask occasional follow-up questions to participants during the discussion. (15 minutes)

V. *Teacher reflection.* The presenting teacher takes a moment to review his or her notes and then reflects aloud on any items he or she chooses. The rest of the team listens without discussion. (5 minutes)

VI. *The debrief.* The facilitator leads a discussion about the experience. (5 minutes)

Note: This is not the NSRF Tuning Protocol, although many other instances of NSRF protocols appear in this book.

---

the presenting teacher and can forestall potential defensiveness, since he or she has decided the focus of the feedback. However, by limiting feedback to an area of the work that is perceived as problematic by the presenting teacher, the focusing question may lead the PLC to inadvertently skirt around larger gaps in the work of which the perceived problem area is but a by-product. I address the advantages and drawbacks of a focusing question more fully in Chapter 9.

Like the Notice and Wonder Protocol, the Tuning Protocol begins with the presenting teacher sharing the context for his or her work, after which team members ask clarifying questions. Participants then offer feedback of two varieties: warm and cool. A discussion of both follows.

Warm and Cool Feedback

Warm feedback communicates to the presenting teacher attributes or components of the work that the teacher offering the feedback believes is particularly strong and worth keeping in the work. High-quality warm feedback is affirming, specific, and free of evaluative language. Less useful warm feedback may be missing one or more of these qualities (see Figure 7.5).

It's not always possible to refrain entirely from evaluative language. Teachers have a natural tendency to offer warm feedback that starts with "I like the way . . . ." Although this is not ideal—unlike the Notice, Like, and Wonder Protocol, which is more of a "starter" protocol, the Tuning Protocol is more advanced and intentionally provides less of a "niceness cushion"—the facilitator can afford to be lenient on this count; it's more important that the feedback be specific. To this end, facilitators can ask pointed follow-up questions to clarify vague warm feedback. For example, a facilitator might respond to the comment "This activity seems very engaging for kids" by asking, "What about it specifically is engaging, do you think?"

Cool feedback, which brings the presenting teacher's attention to gaps in the work, should also be specific (see Figure 7.6 for examples). These gaps may include misalignment to standards, vague expectations of students, ambiguous language, low impact on learning, costly time-benefit ratio, lack of rigor, predominant focus on lower-order thinking, and so on. Unlike warm feedback, cool feedback may have an evaluative bent to it, which is passable as long as the manner in which it is expressed is respectful and nonconfrontational. "I think you should . . . ." can be rephrased less harshly as "She might consider . . . ." During the feedback segment, it is advisable for the presenting teacher to physically move a few feet away from the team and for the

FIGURE 7.5 | Examples of Warm Feedback with Varying Characteristics

Warm Feedback	Affirming	Specific	Free of Evaluative Language
I like the assignment.	x		
The stations make this well differentiated.	x	x	
The rubric contains student-friendly language.	x	x	x

FIGURE 7.6 | Examples of Cool Feedback

- I'm not sure this assignment should be weighted the same as a unit test; maybe if it covered additional standards . . . .
- The second section of this assessment contains questions that are essentially the same. I would suggest varying the level of complexity in this section.
- I wonder if this activity would be better done in pairs rather than groups of four.

participants to refer to the presenting teacher only in the third person. Both of these strategies make it easier for participants to separate the work from the teacher, which helps put at ease both the presenting teacher *and* the PLC members offering feedback.

The Role of Suggestions

In the early days of the Tuning Protocol, when Joseph McDonald and those of us who were part of the Coalition of Essential Schools were field-testing it, we discouraged participants from giving the presenting teacher suggestions about his or her work. The thinking was that if we limited ourselves to pointing out gaps in the work, the presenting teacher would draw his or her own conclusions about what ought to be changed and how. That didn't really work. We learned that to truly be of help to the presenting teacher, PLC members needed to offer suggestions as well as point out gaps. We also learned that presenting teachers genuinely appreciated the suggestions, especially because they were the ones to decide which suggestions they would implement.

The presenting teacher is not the only one to benefit from incorporating suggestions during the feedback segment. Accompanying cool feedback with suggestions tends to be much easier for PLC members than merely offering the feedback; they feel more comfortable sharing feedback when they can also volunteer ideas. That said, suggestions shouldn't *replace* cool feedback, and if a teacher has cool feedback to share but no related suggestions, it is important for him or her to share that feedback regardless. Although suggestions can be tremendously helpful, they are always optional.

Facilitating the Tuning Protocol

When leading a team through the steps of the Tuning Protocol, facilitators should take pains to preserve the safety of the presenting teacher. Paying attention to the body language of the presenting teacher will help the facilitator glean information about the presenter's emotional well-being and anticipate trouble before it arises. Teachers on the team should be aware of the *impact* of their words, not just their words' *intent*. Reminding participants of this before the feedback segment can help, as can asking them to write down cool feedback before sharing it—something I always insist on members doing in my PLCs. Writing down cool feedback first compels team members to think about the words they will use to communicate the feedback. If a team member shares cool feedback that is too pointed or harshly worded, the facilitator must immediately respond. In such instances, I tend to say something like, "Hold on a second. John, could you rephrase that? If I were sitting where Cheryl [presenting teacher] is, I might hear that differently from how I think you mean it." Just a little intervention on the part of the facilitator can defuse the potentially explosive effects of an off-putting comment.

During the teacher reflection segment of the Tuning Protocol, the presenting teacher reflects aloud on the feedback he or she has heard. I generally preface this segment by saying to the presenting teacher, "Cheryl, please take a moment to look over the notes you have taken, and when you're ready, reflect on any you choose. Don't feel as though you have to respond to each item. And remember: this is a reflection, not a defense." Frontloading this step with such a comment helps curb any temptation on the presenting teacher's part to respond defensively to the cool feedback. Sometimes the presenting teacher feels the need to clarify a misunderstanding, which is fine. As facilitator, listen for reflections indicating that the presenting teacher will take a suggestion and modify his or her work in some way based on the feedback. If I don't hear any sign of this in the reflection, I ask, "What changes will you implement based on comments you heard from the team?" The idea is not to put the presenting teacher on the spot, but to encourage her to think about what she's willing to change and to show some commitment to doing so by announcing it to her team. Along those same lines, I always tell the presenting teacher at the end of the reflection segment, "We look forward to hearing about changes you make to this work at a future meeting." Of course, it's important to then follow through by earmarking five minutes at the beginning of a subsequent PLC meeting for Cheryl to update the team on the improvements she has made to her work. This not only provides an element of accountability for Cheryl but also confirms to the rest of the team members that the work they do matters: their meetings precipitate real actions that directly benefit real students.

The Tuning Protocol takes some practice, so take heart if the first time feels awkward. The second time a PLC does a Tuning Protocol is better than the first. The second time a PLC does a Tuning Protocol after talking about how the first one went is *a lot* better than the first, so remember: ***Debrief. Debrief. Debrief.*** The following Fly on the Wall shows how our 8th grade social studies PLC does with its second Tuning Protocol.

FLY ON THE WALL

The Scene:
Bruce's Flashy Poster

What Happened

This is the team's second experience looking at teacher work using the Tuning Protocol. The first time the PLC used the protocol, Cassandra presented her teacher work, and it was a positive experience for all members of the team. Cassandra gained new insights and ideas from her colleagues' feedback and suggestions, and it was clear from the debrief that everyone thought it was a productive meeting.[1]

This time, Bruce has brought a project that he has assigned to students in his State History class for the last three years. The project requires students to choose a notable figure in the state's history, research his or her contributions, and then present the findings to the class dressed up as the historical figure. Bruce assigns this project in February—African American History Month—and encourages students to choose an African American figure as their subject. The project has been warmly received by students and the community at large, and students look forward to dressing up on presentation day. One year, the local news came to do a story on the students' presentations.[2]

After Bruce explains the project requirements and passes out several related handouts, the team moves on to clarifying questions, which Bruce answers succinctly, as Angie had advised:

Devin: The handout says four class periods for this. Does that include the presentations?

Bruce: Yeah, the students work in class for two days, and then we have two days of presentations.

Cassandra: Just curious—do many kids choose an African American subject?[3]

Bruce: Not really. Maybe one or two in each class.

Evelyn: How do you know that the kids aren't just learning about their one person, but learning from the other presentations as well?

(continued)

Before Bruce can answer, Angie forms a *T* with her hands and interrupts:[4]

Angie: Hold on a sec here. I'm not sure Evelyn's question is a *clarifying* question. It *is* a good *probing* question and one I think we should revisit during the discussion segment of the protocol. Are there any other clarifying questions?

Next comes the warm feedback segment, during which team members mention positive attributes of the project:

Cassandra: This project offers a significant level of student choice.

Evelyn (piggybacking on Cassandra): Yes, and that helps make it so engaging for kids.

Devin: I think the kids will remember the information a lot better than if they just wrote a paper.[5]

The warm feedback continues for four more minutes. After giving the team a final chance to offer warm feedback, Angie moves the PLC to cool feedback. At first, there is a significant stretch of silence. Eventually, Cassandra, thinking of the "time-benefit analysis" dimension of the Planning Protocol Rubric (see Figure 10.1, p. 121), breaks the ice:

Cassandra: I'm wondering if four days is a long time to spend on this one standard—actually, just part of the standard.

Angie: I was thinking that, too. Maybe Bruce could have the kids do this in pairs. That could shorten the time students need in class to work on it.

Devin: Yeah, and the presentations would take half as long, right, because there would be half as many.

Angie: Right. That brings the whole time frame down to two days: one for classwork and one for presenting.

Evelyn: I worry about students not really learning about any figures except the one they researched. How can Bruce get the kids to take the other students' presentations seriously, and learn about the other figures?

Cassandra: I think I would give a written quiz on all of the figures a day or so after the presentations.

Devin: Or even just a few figures. He could randomly choose which ones to include in the quiz.

Angie: So I think we agree that Bruce needs to ensure students learn about the figures they did not choose. What about assessing this?[6] Bruce mentions a checklist with points for each item, but I wonder if he could expand on that.

Cassandra: I think he needs a rubric for the whole assignment.

Several minutes pass as the team shares possible dimensions and attributes (e.g., weighting the dimensions) of a rubric.[7] Many remarks build off another member's remark in the exchange:

Evelyn: What about the shy kids who hate this kind of thing—especially *dressing up* to present?

Angie: That's another good reason to have students work in pairs. This could really benefit those kids, Evelyn.

The cool feedback segment winds down shortly thereafter, and Angie guides the team through the final two steps of the protocol: teacher reflection and team debrief.[8]

What's Worth Noting

[1]Just one successful experience looking at teacher work, in which the presenting teacher benefits from his or her colleagues' insights in a safe environment, can open up other team members' willingness to bring in work.

[2]It is always dangerous for a teacher to bring his or her best work or favorite project unless he or she truly believes it contains gaps or shortcomings that the team can help remedy.

[3]There may be more here than a clarifying question, since the information gained by asking it doesn't clarify anything. Angie is smart to let it go and not question Cassandra's motive for asking it.

[4]Angie knows how important it is to immediately intercept questions that are inappropriate during the clarifying questions segment, such as those that question the merits of some aspect of the work. She does this skillfully, and manages to validate Evelyn in the process.

(continued)

[5]This is not terribly specific warm feedback, but it is affirming. Devin is a practical, concrete-sequential thinker—like many teachers in PLCs.

[6]Angie asks a question to steer the team to focus on a significant omission in the work. She does not give her opinion of what is needed, but turns that back to the PLC to discuss and explore.

[7]Many teachers mistake a list of items with point values for an authentic rubric that includes descriptors for each dimension. Discussing possible elements for Bruce's rubric indirectly advances other teammates' knowledge of rubric writing—another example of the power of *constructing community knowledge*.

[8]Assuming Bruce makes the changes he reported he would make during the teacher presentation segment of the protocol, there is no question that the work will get better. Without the PLC's help, how many more years might Bruce have assigned this same project, unchanged and with limited impact on learning?

Summing Up

If PLCs did nothing but look deeply at their work and the work of their students, the quality and quantity of student learning would increase. I can think of no more important way for a PLC to spend its meeting time. Yet too often, teacher teams—and even popular models of the PLC process—get stuck in the weeds of writing SMART goals and planning instructional minutiae.

But how does a PLC prioritize which body of student or teacher work should be looked at? Whether they're looking at student or teacher work, PLCs would be remiss if their choices of which work to review weren't at least in part determined by reviewing student data. In Chapter 8, we'll examine the fine art of facilitating data discussions.

8 | FACILITATING DISCUSSIONS OF DATA

Teachers in an authentic PLC are in the habit of regularly reviewing and discussing student and teacher data. Discussing data is an important precursor to designing instructional plans of action to address areas of need. This is the hard part; to be sure, schools and teachers have become well versed in looking at the data, but the real challenge for teacher teams is to put that review of the data into actionable steps to improve what the data are saying needs improving in the classroom. I developed the Data Action Model to support PLCs in creating plans of action to respond to any gaps in learning and instruction pinpointed by the data. Although this chapter does touch on this model, we will primarily focus on how to facilitate those important data discussions to ensure that what follows the talk is a plan of action that can truly make a difference in student learning. (For specifics on how this model works, see *How Teachers Can Turn Data into Action* [Venables, 2014]).

If the conversations that precede action are superficial or vague approximations of instructional or learning gaps and their root causes, the consequent action plan stands to be equally shallow and ineffective. Part of the facilitator's job is to maintain the authenticity—and, therefore, the efficacy—of these data discussions. Fortunately, there are tools to assist this effort. In this chapter, we'll explore the Notice and Wonder Protocol for Data as well as an overview of the Data Action Model and take a look at how to troubleshoot some common data discussion pitfalls.

The Notice and Wonder Protocol for Data

An old and versatile friend emerges once again. We have seen the simple yet effective way the Notice and Wonder Protocol fosters meaningful discussions surrounding student and teacher work. It is at least as effective in supporting teachers' discussions of data. In fact, as I noted in Chapter 7, I originally designed this protocol for the purpose of discussing data. The steps of this protocol are outlined in Figure 8.1 (see p. 100).

One of the appealing attributes of this protocol is that it enables teachers to more easily and comfortably discuss topics that are often difficult to talk about. In

FIGURE 8.1 | Notice and Wonder Protocol for Data (v2.0)

Time: 40 minutes

Roles: Facilitator, timekeeper, scribe

Purpose: To look descriptively and inferentially at data

I. Participants are presented with a graph or table of data pertaining to their practice. The data may be displayed on a screen for all to see, or they may be given to each PLC member in hard-copy format. (I prefer the former, since graphs and tables of data are often illustrated in color.)

II. Quietly and individually, participants write three or four Notice Statements based on their observations of the graph or table of data. These statements, which begin with the phrase "I notice that . . . ," must be free of inference, judgment, or speculation; they are factual, based on objective examination of the display, and reflect only what is present in the data. (5 minutes)

III. *Round 1: Notice Statements.* Team members take turns reading aloud one new Notice Statement at a time, *without discussion.* The process continues until all Notice Statements have been shared. (5 minutes)

IV. Quietly and individually, participants write three or four Wonder Statements or question-statements about the data. These statements, which begin with the phrase "I wonder why/if/how/whether . . . ," may or may not relate directly to Notice Statements shared in Round 1. Their intent is to gain insight into what the data suggest, how the data are connected, and what the data imply. (5 minutes)

V. *Round 2: Wonder Statements.* Team members take turns reading aloud one new Wonder Statement at a time while the scribe records the statements on chart paper or types them into a document. This process continues until all Wonder Statements have been shared, *without discussion, except* in cases where the facilitator chooses to ask follow-up questions of a teacher sharing a Wonder Statement or of the whole team. (10 minutes)

VI. *The debrief: Content.* The PLC discusses the data and the statements that have been shared, including possible root causes and connections to classroom instruction, and takes note of additional data that may be needed to gain further insight. (10 minutes)

VII. *The debrief: Process.* The team debriefs the process it has just experienced. (5 minutes)

Source: The Notice and Wonder Protocol for Data (v2.0) is a protocol for looking descriptively and inferentially at data developed by Daniel R. Venables. From D. Venables, *The Practice of Authentic PLCs: A Guide to Effective Teacher Teams,* Corwin, 2011. Copyright 2011 by Corwin. Adapted with permission.

the case of discussing teacher and student work, many teachers feel a natural unease in offering feedback on or suggestions for a colleague's work. In the case of discussing data, teachers' discomfort often stems either from not feeling prepared or knowledgeable enough to interpret data or from being uneasy with "putting students' data out there" for all to see (and silently compare). Regardless of the source of teacher insecurity, the Notice and Wonder Protocol does an efficient job of making such discussions easier. Because Notice Statements are statements of fact based on what is observed in the data, they are impossible to argue with, provided that the facilitator does his or her job in calling out Notice Statements that don't fit the requirements. Because they are not disputable or controversial, they tend to be more palatable to even the most defensive teachers hearing them.

By contrast, Wonder Statements by their nature reflect a degree of speculation and inference. It is during the Wonder round of the Notice and Wonder Protocol that discussion moves from what *is* to what *could be*. Herein lies much of the protocol's power: conversations wondering *what if* are necessary antecedents to making solid plans for real action.

As is the case with the Notice and Wonder Protocol for looking at student and teacher work, some Wonder Statements are higher-level than others in their potential to illuminate important learning and instructional gaps. Wonder Statements that relate to the source of the data (e.g., an assessment) are the least valuable in the grand scheme of things (e.g., "I wonder why *eminent domain* is weighted so heavily in terms of the number of test items"), whereas statements having to do with matters of instruction—particularly instruction that *could* happen rather than instruction that *has* happened (e.g., "I wonder if beginning the unit with a real-world application of exponential growth might be a better sequence")—are most powerful in leading the team to identify gaps and eventually design a Data Action Plan.

The Data Action Model

The Data Action Model is a teacher-friendly, step-by-step process for reviewing and responding to student data. Teams begin by examining existing data. Then, driven by an Exploratory Question that they themselves craft, team members find evidence or artifacts to help fine-tune their understanding of what they perceive to be student learning gaps, link those learning gaps to corresponding instructional gaps, and set a Target Learning Goal and a Data Action Plan to fix those gaps. The process culminates with an evaluation of the Data Action Plan based on a metric that the team determined when it first set its Target Learning Goal. The process happens in cycles of five data meetings (see Figure 8.2, p. 102) that span a period of approximately seven to nine weeks, or a typical marking period. The model delineates exactly what steps should be accomplished by the PLC at each data meeting.

The Data Action Model is based on the principle that if teachers thoroughly understand what is happening with regard to student learning gaps, they can fix them. Although a lengthy exploration of the model is beyond the scope of this book, I recommend that PLCs use the model to frame their data discussions. *How Teachers Can Turn Data into Action* (Venables, 2014) provides a comprehensive guide to implementing the model.

FIGURE 8.2 | The Data Action Model at a Glance

Data Meeting 1: Reviewing Existing Data and Asking Questions

    1. Review existing data.
    2. Ask Exploratory Questions.
    3. Decide who will bring what.

Data Meeting 2: Triangulating the Data

    1. Triangulate additional data.

Data Meeting 3: Determining Gaps and Goals

    1. Identify learning gaps.
    2. Identify instructional gaps.
    3. Set a Target Learning Goal.
    4. Decide on an evaluation metric.

Data Meeting 4: Planning for Action

    1. Review strategies and activities.
    2. Develop a Data Action Plan.

Data Meeting 5: Evaluating Success and Determining Next Steps

    1. Evaluate effectiveness of implementation.
    2. Determine the next course of action.

One important feature of this model is that everything happens at the PLC level. Every step—from exploring the original macrodata (e.g., Common Core assessment data, end-of-course data, district benchmark data) to examining smaller microdata artifacts (e.g., formative assessment results, homework, classwork), setting the Target Learning Goal, creating and implementing the Data Action Plan, and finally evaluating how successful the plan was in reaching the goal—is led by the teacher team. Granting teachers ownership, voice, and choice in nearly every step along the way promotes significant buy-in among team members.

Principals, too, tend to appreciate that teachers own every part of the process. They quickly see that when their teachers are empowered to conduct data analyses, identify gaps based on evidence, and develop action plans that they themselves will implement and monitor in their classrooms, instructional improvements necessarily happen as part and parcel of the Data Action Model's structure. There is no top-down decision that could ever match the power of the Data Action Model when used with fidelity.

Troubleshooting 10 Data Discussion Pitfalls

Even when they use the best model for reviewing and responding to data, teachers can still have data discussions that don't go deep enough. If this happens, any subsequent plan of action or attempt at implementing the plan may not be sufficient in filling student learning gaps. In that event, the team will have spent a lot of time and energy tilling soil that never yielded crops. It is therefore essential that facilitators do everything in their power to ensure that when teachers are noticing and wondering and determining their plan of action, the prerequisite data discussions are fertile ones.

To help PLC facilitators preemptively troubleshoot potential data discussion pitfalls, I created the activity in Figure 8.3. We use it during our Grapple Data Institute training for PLC facilitators, and participants regularly testify to its usefulness. It is not possible to anticipate every data discussion pitfall, but these 10 scenarios are the most common ones I've seen in schools with which I've worked. This activity encourages facilitators to think about how to handle these situations before they arise.

FIGURE 8.3 | Potential Data Discussion Pitfalls*: How Would You Handle Them?

---

*aka *Opportunities*

Time: 35 minutes

I. Participants pair off (*A, B*) and access a virtual 10-sided die (e.g., by downloading a dice-rolling app like Dice Roller or The Game Dice Roller or visiting http://www.roll-dice-online.com).

II. *Rounds.* (10 minutes each, 20 minutes total)

1. Participant *A* rolls the virtual decahedron die to determine which pitfall of the 10 listed in the table below he or she will troubleshoot. Participant *A* has five minutes to collect his or her thoughts *and* share with Participant *B* how he or she would respond. Participant *B* keeps track of the time and does not speak.
2. Participant *B* has two minutes to respond to Participant *A*'s solution. Participant *A* keeps track of the time and does not speak.
3. Participants *A* and *B* have three minutes to articulate in the table their best collective thinking on how to address the pitfall.
4. Participants repeat steps 1–3, this time switching roles, and rolling again if they get the same pitfall as the first time.

III. *Discussion.* Pairs return to the table and share their pitfalls and solutions with other pairs. (10 minutes)

(continued)

FIGURE 8.3 | Potential Data Discussion Pitfalls: How Would You Handle Them? (continued)

IV. *Large-group debrief.* (5 minutes)

Pitfall	What would you ask, say, or do?
1. Focus of data conversation shifts to issues over which the team has no control.	
2. Focus of data conversation is on trivial, relatively unimportant observations.	
3. The team is quick to blame students and reluctant to accept responsibility for learning gaps.	
4. Data conversation becomes micro-focused on one particular student or test item.	
5. Focus of data conversation shifts to skills students "should have acquired before this year."	
6. Team jumps prematurely to proposing solutions.	
7. Focus of data conversation shifts to items unrelated to the data at hand.	
8. Focus of data conversation is on secondary symptoms of an undiscussed primary issue.	
9. Team is celebratory and self-congratulatory about what is working.	
10. Focus of data conversation shifts to sustained sentiments of helplessness and pessimism.	

Source: Pitfalls come from "10 Potential Data Discussion Pitfalls," by D.R. Venables and N. Cooperman, 2013. © 2013 by Daniel R. Venables and Teaching Matters, Inc. Reprinted with permission.

As a final note, it is important to keep in mind that the tasks in which authentic PLCs engage are not happening in a vacuum, nor are they independent, unrelated endeavors; how the PLC spends its coveted time should be driven by needs that are revealed by the data. Otherwise, each meeting has little to do with previous or subsequent meetings, and the whole PLC experience becomes a series of independent endeavors quilted together with no driving force or central purpose.

9 | FACILITATING DISCUSSIONS SURROUNDING A TEACHER OR TEAM DILEMMA

There is more to teaching than designing lessons and writing assessments. In fact, because there are so many interconnected, moving parts to the endeavor, there are lots of places for teachers to experience jams that interfere with the otherwise smoothly functioning cogs of teaching. When such dilemmas occur, it is not surprising that teachers who are members of authentic PLCs turn to their teams for support. After all, authentic PLCs hold at their core a commitment to helping each of their teachers succeed; if a teacher is experiencing a dilemma that is interfering with his or her teaching, it is fitting that the team help. How many of us of a certain age wish PLCs had been around early in our careers, when teaching-related challenges cropped up around every corner? Wouldn't it have been nice to have such a support system—and to have tools and a structure for such support?

To be clear, PLCs are not a forum for solving problems in members' personal lives. This is an important distinction; it is never advisable for a PLC to spend its precious time on issues not related to teaching and learning. PLCs provide the perfect venue, however, for helping teachers who face specific classroom dilemmas or more general issues related to their practice. Dilemmas worthy of PLC support have the following four characteristics:

1. The dilemma is specific and directly relates to some aspect of teaching or learning.
2. The dilemma is significant enough that it may be causing secondary issues or dilemmas.
3. The dilemma has no clear resolution in sight.
4. The dilemma's solution, once identified, does not require *other* people to change their behavior (Venables, 2011).

Examples of "worthy" dilemmas include the following:

- A teacher is having ongoing difficulty with a student despite several (failed) attempts to manage him.

- A special education teacher in an inclusion classroom is experiencing friction with a classroom teacher with whom she works.
- A teacher becomes aware of systemic cheating that occurred on a major assessment in her class.

Despite their brevity and lack of detail, these dilemmas reflect specific rather than general situations; each issue involves a specific student, a specific teacher, or a specific assessment. Team members can fill in the details surrounding such dilemmas during the early segments of whichever protocol they decide to use to discuss the dilemma. We'll discuss two such protocols in this chapter: the Consultancy Protocol, which is ideal for resolving individual teacher dilemmas; and the Shared Dilemma Protocol, which a PLC can use to address a dilemma affecting the entire team.

The Consultancy Protocol

The Consultancy Protocol is a particularly effective tool for helping PLC members troubleshoot issues that are interfering with their teaching and students' learning. First developed by educators with the Coalition of Essential Schools and the National School Reform Faculty, it is well suited to helping a teacher think about a dilemma from varying vantage points, thereby driving the teacher to solve his or her own issue. The steps of a 40-minute Consultancy Protocol are outlined in Figure 9.1. (Note: The text of Figure 9.1 is a compilation and adaptation of the earliest version of the Consultancy Protocol and Consultancy Protocol Overview from the National School Reform Faculty. The NSRF now teaches the Consultancy differently.)

The Consultancy Protocol opens with the presenting teacher sharing his or her dilemma, the context for the dilemma, and other information that provides the rest of the team with a clear picture of the issue. Often, the presenting teacher concludes the segment with a framing or focus question that highlights the issue and where he or she would like help. This can be a bit tricky; sometimes a focus question is too restrictive in terms of what it permits team members to question or discuss. The worst-case scenario is that the focus question directs the team's attention to the wrong issue—which, in many cases, is part of the original problem: the presenting teacher has been focusing on the wrong issue and, as a result, has attempted ineffective solutions. When the presenting teacher's perception of the dilemma—including its causes and possible solutions—is off the mark, his or her focus question based on that misperception may limit how helpful the team can be in solving the problem. As facilitators, we want the discussion to be as good as it can be—not just as good as the focus question is. If a focus question is well written and gets to the heart of the issue, then it can be beneficial. But if it is poorly or hurriedly crafted or fails to accurately pinpoint the central dilemma, it's best not to use it at all.

FIGURE 9.1 | Consultancy Protocol

Purpose: To open up people's minds to new ways of thinking about a problem or issue related to teaching and learning

Roles: Facilitator, presenting teacher(s), timekeeper

Pre-work for the Presenting Teacher: Writing About the Dilemma

Consider the dilemma. The dilemma should be an issue with which you are struggling, that has a way to go before being resolved, that is up to you to control, and that is crucial to your work. It is important that your problem be authentic and fresh—that is, not already solved or nearly solved.

Write a short paragraph summarizing the dilemma. Use the following questions to guide your writing:

1. Why is this a dilemma for you? Why is this dilemma important to you?
2. If you could take a snapshot of this dilemma, what would you/we see?
3. What have you already done to try to remedy or manage the dilemma?
4. What have been the results of those attempts?
5. Who do you hope changes? Who do you hope will take action to resolve this dilemma? If your answer is not *you,* you need to change your focus. The dilemma you present should be about *your* practice, behaviors, beliefs, and assumptions, not someone else's.
6. What do you assume to be true about this dilemma? How have these assumptions influenced your thinking about the dilemma?

The Consultancy Protocol

Time: 40 minutes

I. *Presenter overview.* The presenter gives an overview of the dilemma for the team to consider. (3 minutes)

II. *Clarifying questions.* (5 minutes)

- Participants ask clarifying questions of the presenter. Clarifying questions can be answered with facts.
- If the questions are not clarifying, they should be rephrased so that they are or saved for the subsequent participant discussion.

III. *Probing questions.* (7 minutes)

- Participants ask probing questions of the presenter. The purpose of probing questions is to expand the presenter's thinking about the issue to jump-start analysis of the dilemma.
- The presenter may choose not to respond to a question by saying, "Pass on that one" or "Let me think about that."

IV. *Participant discussion.* (15 minutes)

- The presenter withdraws from the group, taking notes on the participants' discussion of the dilemma. Participants talk with one another without addressing the presenter.

(continued)

FIGURE 9.1 | Consultancy Protocol (continued)

- Participants may describe actions that the presenter could take, but they should not feel as though they need to arrive at a solution to the dilemma.
- Suggested questions for the facilitator to ask to get the discussion going include the following:
  - What did we hear?
  - What didn't we hear that we think might be relevant?
  - What assumptions seem to be operating?
  - What questions does the dilemma raise for us?
  - What do we think about the dilemma?
  - What might we do or try if faced with a similar dilemma? What have we done in similar situations?

V. *Presenter reflection.* (5 minutes)

- Referring to notes taken during the participant discussion, the presenter reflects on the participants' comments and their effect on his or her thinking.
- It is particularly important for the presenter to share new insights that the discussion has provided.

VI. *Debrief.* The facilitator leads the group in a discussion of the protocol process. (5 minutes)

Source: This protocol was developed in conjunction with the Coalition of Essential Schools and the Annenberg Institute for School Reform, which became the National School Reform Faculty. The NSRF now recommends one or more variations on this protocol. Special permission has been received to reproduce the Consultancy Protocol from NSRF. See http://www.nsrfharmony.org or call 812-330-2702 for more resources and to learn about coaches' training to use NSRF resources most effectively.

Clarifying and Probing Questions

Once the presenting teacher has shared the necessary background information, participants—who have been silently taking notes up to this point—are permitted to ask clarifying questions. PLC members ask clarifying questions to acquire additional details or context surrounding the issue so that they more fully understand the dilemma. Clarifying questions are nonjudgmental and nonsuggestive, and they do not attempt to achieve anything close to a solution. Because clarifying questions are factually based, the presenting teacher's answers tend to be brief. Figure 9.2 includes examples of clarifying questions and answers.

If a participant asks a clarifying question and the presenting teacher pauses before answering, it could be an indicator that the question was not clarifying. The second example in Figure 9.2 occupies the gray area between a suggestion and a clarifying question. Given the brevity and factual nature of the response, it was more likely a clarifying question. However, if the presenting teacher had answered, "No, but that's a good idea," that would indicate that the question was received as a suggestion rather than a point of clarification. Facilitators should be watchful of clarifying

FIGURE 9.2 | Examples of Clarifying Questions and Answers

Clarifying Question	Answer
When did you first notice this?	Just after Thanksgiving.
Have you contacted the parents?	I tried, but the number on file with the school is disconnected.
Do you know if Mr. Baldwin has spoken to him?	He has not.

questions that attempt to do more than merely clarify while recognizing that there is always a gray area and that they should go with their gut in facilitating this segment of the protocol.

Probing questions, which make up the next segment of the Consultancy Protocol, are asked not for the benefit of the teacher asking the question but for the benefit of the presenting teacher. Probing questions give the presenting teacher new ways of thinking about the dilemma, push him or her to think more expansively about the issue, and often bring his or her underlying assumptions to the surface. This last characteristic can be transformative for the presenting teacher, as it forces an honest look at the issue and a questioning way of thinking about it. Good probing questions do not judge or evaluate, and, as such, generally do not put the presenting teacher on the defensive. Rather, they push the team's thinking to a deeper level where, most often, a solution to the problem resides.

Probing questions are not leading questions. During the subsequent participant discussion segment of the protocol, the team makes suggestions and discusses possible solutions, but these are not appropriate during the probing questions segment. Questions that are thinly disguised suggestions do no probing whatever; they simply direct the teacher to a call for action. For example, the question "Do you think it would be a good idea to move Nathan to the front of the class?" is really saying, "I have an idea: move Nathan to the front of the class." It may be a truly marvelous idea, but it belongs in the discussion segment of the protocol, where suggestions are appropriate, rather than disguised as a question, which can be off-putting to the presenting teacher. A probing question that gets at the same notion might be "How do you think the arrangement of the room might be influencing Nathan's behavior?" ***Do ask, don't tell.*** Compelling the presenting teacher to think about an aspect of the dilemma is not the same as telling her what we think she should do. The question stems listed in Figure 3.1 (p. 40) provide some good jumping-off points for probing questions.

Often, probing questions spawn follow-up questions, depending on how the presenting teacher answers the former. For this reason, facilitators should remind team members to leave space between the probing question just asked and the one they are about to ask because there may be a follow-up question coming from the first teacher. Many times, it is the follow-up questions that move the team's thinking to the most useful places. Seasoned facilitators are very good at pursuing useful follow-up questions and favor these consistent lines of questioning over a crazy quilt of disparate probing questions. Figure 9.3 includes several examples of probing questions and follow-up questions.

FIGURE 9.3 | Examples of Probing Questions and Follow-Up Questions

Probing Question	Possible Follow-Up Question
If you had to pinpoint the biggest contributing factor to this situation, what would it be?	Why?
What do you think would happen if the reverse were true?	Then what?
What would you suggest to me, if this were my problem?	How can *you* do that?

Successful application of the Consultancy Protocol unites the PLC in new and deep ways. A teacher who chooses to present his or her dilemma to the team is showing a degree of vulnerability that necessitates a level of trust among team members. The protocol itself ramps up the team's level of trust in a way that cannot be achieved through more mundane tasks like writing common assessments. Even better, once teams have established a bedrock of trust, even if they're relatively new to protocols, they can experience the Consultancy Protocol. Finally, as is the case with most of the protocols put into service by authentic PLCs, all of the teachers on the team who participate in the Consultancy Protocol personally benefit from the experience. Each teacher dilemma discussed has parallels to other issues and dilemmas experienced by other members of the PLC. The following Fly on the Wall shows how our 8th grade social studies PLC addresses a teacher dilemma using the Consultancy Protocol.

FLY ON THE WALL

The Scene:
Evelyn's Dilemma

What Happened

In this meeting, Evelyn has brought a dilemma she's experiencing in the classroom to her team (see elements of "worthy" dilemmas, p. 105). To help Evelyn with her issue, Angie suggests that the team use the Consultancy Protocol.

Because this is the first time the team is using the Consultancy Protocol, Angie begins the meeting by asking her team to read a short excerpt on probing questions.[1] When participants finish the short reading, she begins.

Angie: Being able to ask good probing questions takes a little practice. For now, do your best; we will learn together as we go.[2] Please keep in mind that we're not making suggestions during the probing questions segment. There will be a separate segment in the protocol for making suggestions.

After Angie solicits a volunteer to keep time, the protocol starts, with Evelyn giving the necessary background information on her dilemma. Her dilemma centers on a special education teacher, Felicia, who co-teaches in Evelyn's 2nd and 5th period social studies classes. Evelyn describes the tension that arises when the two teachers are in the classroom working with the students. According to Evelyn, Felicia is not helpful in working with struggling students, often engages in distracting side conversations with students while Evelyn is teaching, and generally has an unpleasant attitude toward Evelyn. Evelyn wants the relationship to function better but isn't sure what to do. She ends her overview of the situation with a focus question: *What can I do to improve my working relationship with Felicia so that students can better benefit from having both of us in the classroom?*[3]

The team moves to clarifying questions:

Bruce: How long has this been going on?

Devin: What have you already tried?

Cassandra: Are the kids picking up on this tension?

(continued)

Angie: Do you work with a different special education teacher during 3rd and 4th periods?

Evelyn responds to these fact-based questions with brief answers, as Angie has suggested.

Next come probing questions. Angie reminds the team that, unlike clarifying questions, these questions are asked for the benefit of the person answering the questions. Before they begin, Angie turns to Evelyn:

Angie: These questions are to help you think more deeply about your issue, perhaps in new ways. Please realize that there is no evaluation or judgment in these questions; we are asking them to help you.[4] Your answers will probably be longer than those for the clarifying questions. Remember that you can always pass by saying something like "I'd have to think more about that." (To the group) Remember, team, allow for pauses between questions, since someone may wish to ask a follow-up question.

The team members then ask Evelyn some initial probing questions:

Cassandra: How do you think Felicia would describe your working relationship with her?

Devin: Have you talked to Mark [the assistant principal] about it?[5]

Angie: What are your expectations for how Felicia should be contributing to the class?

Bruce: What are the nonnegotiables for you?

Another eight questions follow. Evelyn gives each one an earnest answer. When the probing questions segment is finished, Angie asks Evelyn to move away from the group a bit and take notes on the participant discussion.

Angie starts out the discussion segment by asking her team two questions prescribed in the Consultancy Protocol: "What did we hear?" and "What didn't we hear that we think might be relevant?" Once the discussion takes on a life of its own, Angie relies less on the prescribed questions.[6]

During the participant discussion, the team makes several good suggestions to guide Evelyn through her next steps. Team members bounce ideas off one another as they refine and add to the suggestions offered. Throughout this segment, Evelyn's head is down as she quietly takes notes in a notebook.[7]

Angie then guides the team to the presenter's reflection:

Angie: (To Evelyn) During this segment, Evelyn, you can comment on any of the things you heard during our discussion. Don't feel as though you need to comment on all of them. And remember, this segment is a reflection, not a defense. We are particularly interested in how we may have helped and what your next steps might include.[8]

Evelyn quickly reviews her notes and begins:

Evelyn: Thank you, everybody, for all your thoughts. I already feel like a weight is being lifted off my shoulders. [She glances down at her notes.] I think you all are right: I really do need to have a conversation with Felicia. I never really thought about my expectations for how we would work together until you asked. Sharing those and asking Felicia for her expectations, as Cassandra suggested[9], is a great place to start this conversation. In addition to that, I think the room setup changes that Bruce suggested are probably a good idea. Angie, I love the suggestion to set up a specific time each week to plan with Felicia. I think that alone will help things. I'm not sure how I feel about the suggestion to invite Mark [the assistant principal] to be present at this conversation; maybe if this doesn't work, but I think his presence may jeopardize productivity and put Felicia on the defensive.

Evelyn continues her reflection for several more minutes, concluding with a second expression of gratitude to her team. Angie thanks Evelyn for being brave enough to share her dilemma and then moves to the debrief segment of the protocol.

What's Worth Noting

[1]Facilitators can offset potential difficulties in any new task—particularly new protocols—by anticipating them and providing the team with additional information upfront, such as doing a short reading. This small time investment can pay big dividends in producing a higher-quality experience than might otherwise be the case.

[2]Angie's encouragement is frequent and sincere.

(continued)

[3]It is not essential for the presenting teacher to offer a focus question. Such a question can help the team home in on what the presenting teacher wants out of the experience so long as the question gets to the heart of the matter in clear terms. If the focus question is poorly phrased, the team may be confused about the dilemma or the teacher's goals. And if the presenting teacher presents the dilemma clearly, a focus question may be unnecessary. If the teacher does offer a focus question, it should be written down by all team members, and the facilitator should refer to it during the discussion segment of the protocol.

[4]From her training as a PLC facilitator, Angie knows that probing questions can sometimes trigger defensiveness on the part of the presenting teacher. Because she is also aware that Evelyn gets defensive at times, she preemptively addresses this issue before the probing questions segment.

[5]Devin's question is more of a suggestion or a clarifying question than it is a probing question. However, it is not a *harmful* question, so Angie is wise to leave it alone.

[6]The questions in step IV of the Consultancy Protocol should serve as a guide for the facilitator; not all of the questions need be asked, nor are they comprehensive. My personal preference is to ask the first two questions and then see where the conversation goes after that.

[7]Most often, the presenting teacher will take notes on a laptop, although a few prefer to record contributions the old-fashioned way. The laptop can provide a physical barrier between the presenting teacher and the team in a way that helps them separate the work or issue from the teacher.

[8]Angie consistently does a nice job setting up each segment of the protocol. This statement tacitly reminds team members that they are there to help and Evelyn that she is expected to implement some of the ideas that emerge.

[9]It is common for presenting teachers to "credit" colleagues who offer ideas that the presenting teacher likes and plans to try. In a perfect world, she might more neutrally reflect without referring to the originator of the idea, since the goal is to focus on the idea rather than on the teacher; but in practice, crediting the teacher whose idea it is seems to flow naturally and does no harm. In a way, it can validate the contributing teacher and strengthen the team.

Shared Dilemma Protocol

There are times when the PLC as a whole faces a dilemma or an issue that needs to be addressed lest it impede the PLC's ability to move forward. Sometimes the dilemma is of a personal nature (e.g., tension between two members of the PLC), other times it is an instructional or assessment-related dilemma, and still other times it centers on a policy or even a parent. In any of these cases, if the dilemma is not resolved, it becomes something of an elephant in the room, and the work of the PLC becomes tainted or, worse, halted altogether. A PLC may face a recurring shared dilemma year after year until the team decides to address it head-on. Figure 9.4 includes several such examples of shared dilemmas and their respective domains.

In each of the examples in Figure 9.4, the dilemma is shared by the whole team, is significant, is as yet unsolved, and is affecting corollary actions and decisions to be

FIGURE 9.4 | Examples of Shared Dilemmas

Domain of the Dilemma	Shared Dilemma
PLC	*What norms?* Members of the PLC are not following the list of norms they agreed to when the team first formed.
Assessment	*Test security.* All Biology students take the same common formative assessments that the Biology PLC designs, although the honors class's versions of the assessments contain some additional, more challenging questions. Because they move more quickly in class, the honors Biology students take the assessment a week or so before the rest of the Biology students. Consequently, the regular Biology kids are getting test items leaked to them from the honors kids.
Instruction	*Didactic differences.* Members of the Grade 5 PLC are of one mind when it comes to innovation in the classroom and teaching students 21st century skills. This mindset and teachers' resulting practice are at odds with much of the standardized testing their students must endure. This dilemma has also created tension between the team and the school's administrators.
Larger Community	*Pushy parents.* The Math PLC is finding that its criteria for placing students in honors math classes are frequently being overridden by parents who seek to push their kids into the honors class in cases where the Math PLC has made a recommendation against it.

made by the team. In each case, the issues are quite commonplace; I have seen each of these play out in real schools. Likely solutions to these dilemmas require PLC members to take actionable steps but do not require other contributing agents to change their behaviors. To solve their dilemma, team members need to own it and decide on action that they themselves can achieve independently of other people.

The Shared Dilemma Protocol, originally developed by my friend and colleague Cari Begin, is an effective tool for bringing the team's focus and energy to the dilemma at hand. The version of the Shared Dilemma Protocol featured in Figure 9.5 is one I revised from Cari's original. The time required to complete it is 45 minutes.

FIGURE 9.5 | Shared Dilemma Protocol (v2.0)

Purpose: Teacher teams often experience dilemmas or problems that are pervasive across a grade level or subject area. This protocol provides a structured way for teacher teams to start the process of solving a shared dilemma or problem that is within their sphere of influence or control.

Time: 45 minutes

Roles: Facilitator (explains each step, moderates, and participates), timekeeper, recorder

Pre-work: A specific dilemma that most members of the PLC face is identified in a prior meeting.

I. *The dilemma.* The facilitator presents the common dilemma to the group. Participants may ask a few clarifying questions to ensure that everyone has necessary information. (3 minutes)

II. *Probing questions.* (17 minutes)

   1. Participants are given five minutes to quietly write one probing question that will encourage deeper conversation about the dilemma. During the next two minutes, participants take turns sharing their questions without discussion while the recorder writes them on chart paper or a whiteboard or in a digital format that everyone can see. (7 minutes)

   2. Participants take time to respond to and discuss some or all of the probing questions on the list. The recorder writes the responses on chart paper or a whiteboard or in a digital format. (10 minutes)

III. *Solutions.* (10 minutes)

   1. Participants brainstorm possible solutions. Again, the recorder writes the ideas where everyone can see them. (5 minutes)

   2. Participants engage in an open discussion about the proposed solutions and are encouraged to ask clarifying questions to gain a better understanding of these possible solutions. (5 minutes)

IV. *Next steps.* The facilitator asks questions like "What will we do now based on this discussion? Which solutions should we put into an action plan? Which solutions should we investigate further? Which solutions are we ready to agree to implement?" The recorder takes notes using the chart below to organize ideas. (10 minutes)

FIGURE 9.5 | Shared Dilemma Protocol (v2.0) (continued)

	Description	Timeline	Responsible Party
Solutions requiring investigation			
Solutions to put into action			

V. *Debrief.* (5 minutes)

Source: Protocol first developed by Cari Begin with contributions from Daniel R. Venables to help teacher teams start the process of solving a shared dilemma over which they have control. © 2013 by Cari Begin. Revised by Daniel R. Venables © 2016.

The Shared Dilemma Protocol bears a resemblance to the Consultancy Protocol; the biggest difference is that the whole team owns the dilemma *and* its eventual solution. If the dilemma is not solved outright, it is at least mitigated by the team's collaborative process of experiencing the protocol and taking time to address the situation.

This protocol requires that facilitators proceed with deliberate care, especially when the dilemma revolves around interpersonal dynamics in the team. It is important for facilitators to encourage differing perspectives during the Shared Dilemma Protocol, since they are likely to be a component of the issue. Of course, not all shared dilemmas involve interpersonal issues; many times, the shared dilemma intersects identified learning gaps revealed by data (for example, when students across all of the PLC members' classes are consistently underperforming on a specific standard).

Summing Up

Left unresolved, a teaching-related dilemma—whether owned by an individual teacher or the whole team—can interfere with the growth, dynamics, and productivity of a PLC and have a significant negative effect on classroom instruction. Teachers' ability to function at their highest potential without being hampered by the shackles of an unresolved dilemma is more important than their SMART goals and deserves to be part of an authentic, high-functioning PLC.

10 | FACILITATING COLLABORATIVE PLANNING TIME

Low-functioning PLCs spend most of their meeting time planning *what* they are about to teach in their classrooms and *when* they will "cover" it. Little attention is given to *how* they will teach it. They might write SMART goals and design common formative assessments—as well they should—but when it comes to student learning, their conversations are reactive rather than proactive. They spend adequate time addressing the question "What do we do if our students don't learn?" (DuFour, DuFour, & Eaker, 2008) but less time, if any, asking, "What's the best way to teach this so that our students learn it in the first place?" (Venables, 2011, 2014).

To be sure, conversations about what to teach and when to teach it need to happen; that's just the reality of being part of a team of teachers. The challenge is being able to strike a balance between planning *what* to teach and planning *how* to teach specific content. In this final chapter, we'll explore ways to help PLCs achieve this elusive balance, including vetting instruction and using the Planning Protocol Rubric and the Charrette Protocol.

The Importance of Vetting Instruction

In many schools I visit, teams seem to have an unspoken understanding that the content will be taught essentially the same as it was the previous year, even if that instruction proved to be less than successful. The teams' discussions then focus on matters like which day topic *X* will be taught, when project *Y* will start, or on what day the test will fall, as if those were the only things left to discuss *this* year. This mindset is fundamentally flawed.

Authentic PLCs are in the regular habit of discussing how to teach content, which activities are best to use, and which of last year's less-than-effective activities should be replaced with new ones. I call instructional components that have been thoroughly assessed for their potential to induce a high quantity and quality of learning *vetted instruction*. PLCs can be enormously helpful in vetting instruction, whether they're planning common lessons or looking at one member's work using protocols discussed in Chapter 7. Either way, it's easier to look at the *how* of teaching with the abundance of knowledge and experience a PLC can offer. Even better, discussions surrounding the *how* inevitably bump up against discussions of the *what,* since the latter serve as building blocks of discussions of the *how.* The converse is not true: focusing discussion on *what* we will teach does not necessarily include mention of *how* we will teach it. The *what* is simply no match for the *how.*

Arguably the most valuable aspect of vetting instruction is that it is proactive rather than reactive. Vetting instruction allows us to discuss how we will teach particular content before we have done so; when done thoughtfully, this process can reduce the amount of intervention that is needed down the line for students who didn't learn from our instruction. Schools that *proactively* spend more and higher-quality time discussing how to teach particular content tend to spend less time *reactively* discussing what to do when inadequately vetted methods have failed.

Flashy Poster Syndrome

Early in my teaching career, in the 1980s, I assessed my 9th grade Algebra 1 students' mastery by having them make posters listing and providing examples of various topics covered in class (for example, the Laws of Exponents). The posters were generally beautifully done, with fancy fonts and vibrant images filling neon-colored poster board. One year, about three years into assigning this project, I had students work in pairs to create the posters and then present them to the class. When I asked questions of the pairs toward the end of their presentations, I was dumbstruck by how little students actually knew about their topics. It became disappointingly apparent to me that the project didn't exhibit any learning whatsoever; it was instead a *copyfest* of information straight out of the book, repackaged with flashy window dressing that distracted me from the truth: the assignment demonstrated no real learning or conceptual understanding of the content. I was duped by my own bright idea.

I have since referred to this phenomenon as *Flashy Poster Syndrome*: the act of engaging kids in instructional assignments or assessments that appear wonderful on the surface but lead to or demonstrate no real learning by the students. We have all done it before; the project may manifest itself as a poem, a skit, a 3D model, a Power-Point or an Ignite presentation, a newsletter, or a brochure. To be fair, these projects tend to be very engaging, and they aren't inherently empty; they can be filled with real learning. That's a good thing. But their engaging aspect often ends up becoming the reason for their existence, which is not good. *Engaging* does not automatically imply *rigorous* or *substantive.* For that, we must vet instruction and look more closely and objectively at assignments, assessments, and activities that we are considering implementing in our classrooms. After all, time is short; we surely don't have enough of it to waste nurturing a tree that bears no fruit or, worse, one that bears beach apples.

The Planning Protocol Rubric

So what is the best way to vet instructional methods or assignments? Obviously, student data can help us assess the effectiveness of past instruction, but that's a reactive approach. For never-tried strategies, lessons, and activities that we are considering implementing in the classroom, we need a discussion and vetting process. For this purpose, I developed the Planning Protocol Rubric (see Figure 10.1).

To use the rubric, PLC members individually score the activity across each dimension and then engage in a facilitator-led discussion of how they arrived at their scores. The following section takes a closer look at the dimensions and questions to consider in scoring them.

The Dimensions of the Planning Protocol Rubric

Each dimension of the Planning Protocol Rubric identifies an important characteristic for a lesson component or activity we are considering using with students. A rundown of these dimensions follows.

Alignment to standards. Most teachers would probably agree that if an activity or a lesson component is not aligned to the content standards to which the school or district adheres, it forfeits consideration for implementation, however rich or effective it might be. This is the unfortunate reality in schools today. If an activity is at least partially aligned to standards, questions to consider include *Which component of this lesson best aligns to the standards? Why? What do we think mastery looks like for these standards?*

Impact on learning. After alignment to standards, this is the most important dimension. If I had had a rubric in my early teaching years that forced me to analyze the extent to which "flashy poster" projects facilitated or exhibited authentic learning, I suspect it wouldn't have taken me four years to hit the pause button and rethink such assignments. Although the scoring of this dimension is subjective, teachers can call upon their experience and expertise to speculate how effective they believe the activity will be in terms of student learning. Questions to consider include *How much learning is likely to result from this activity or lesson component? Is the gain significant? Does the activity or component work more effectively for one student group or another? Why?*

Student engagement. Again, there is no "rubric within the rubric" to score this dimension; even teachers with little experience can predict with reasonable accuracy how engaging an activity stands to be with their students.

Depth of Knowledge level. This dimension refers to Webb's Depth of Knowledge Levels (see Webb, Alt, Ely, & Vesperman, 2005), which categorize tasks according to the complexity of thinking they require. Questions to consider include *Are*

FIGURE 10.1 | Planning Protocol Activity with Rubric (v3.0)

Dimension	1	2	3	4
Alignment to Standards	Barely aligned or not aligned	Somewhat aligned	Mostly aligned	Completely aligned
Impact on Learning	Low impact	Medium-low impact	Medium-high impact	High impact
Student Engagement	Low engagement for most students	Moderate engagement for some students	Moderate engagement for most students	High engagement for most students
Depth of Knowledge Level	Recall	Skill/concept	Strategic reasoning	Extended reasoning
Technology Integration	No integration of technology	Some integration of technology	Effective and prominent integration of technology	Effective and innovative integration of technology
Teacher Friendliness		High-maintenance (lots of materials and prep work)	Low-maintenance (few materials or little prep work)	
Rigor and Relevance	Teacher works	Students work	Students think	Students think and work
Differentiation	Not suited for differentiation	Suited for differentiation with fairly significant modifications	Well suited for differentiation with minor modifications	Well suited for differentiation as is, with natural tiers built in
Time-Benefit Analysis	Too much instructional time required for relatively little learning	Questionable amount of time required for expected amount of learning	Amount of time required and amount of learning are commensurate	Small amount of time required for amount of learning that exceeds expectations

(continued)

FIGURE 10.1 | Planning Protocol Activity with Rubric (v3.0) (continued)

Dimension	1	2	3	4
Connections	No connections to previous or future standards or to other subjects	A few genuine connections to other standards or subjects	Genuine connections to other standards and/or subjects embedded in various components	Strong, authentic connections to previous and future standards and to other subjects

Alignment: *Which component of this lesson best aligns to the standards? Why? What do we think mastery looks like for these standards?*

Impact: *How much learning is likely to result from this lesson? Is the gain significant? Where do students typically have trouble with these concepts, and why? Do the activities/ components selected work better for one group or another? Why?*

Depth: *Are students being pushed (and guided) to think on a high level? How do you know? Which components of this lesson push deeper thinking? Do the activities/components selected lend themselves to differentiation? How?*

---

students being pushed (and guided) to think on a high level? How do we know? Which component(s) of this lesson push(es) deeper thinking?

Technology integration. In an era of readying students to function at high levels in the 21st century, it would be remiss to imagine implementing a new lesson component or activity without considering the extent to which it incorporates technology. That's not to say lessons should shoehorn in technology just for the sake of including it. But it is prudent to consider questions like *Can students produce a digital product to meet the requirements? How can the use of apps enhance this activity or lesson? Does this lesson overlook opportunities to capitalize on technological tools? Would technology enhance or detract from student learning here?*

Teacher friendliness. I included this rubric dimension because teachers are very busy people, so the time they spend constructing or compiling physical or digital components of a lesson is relevant. There are only two scoring options— high-maintenance and low-maintenance—to reflect that this dimension is easily scored and not quite as important as other dimensions. The "high-maintenance" score applies to activities or lessons that require considerable prep work (e.g., gathering materials, cutting out components, or loading apps on devices), whereas "low-maintenance" refers to activities with less prep. To be clear, lessons or activities that score high on other dimensions should never be ruled out simply because they may be high-maintenance for teachers. Teacher friendliness is one aspect for consideration, but it's by no means a deciding aspect.

Rigor and relevance. It is possible for a lesson or an activity to have a significant impact on student learning without being rigorous. This dimension prompts a conversation about the level of work and thought that the activity requires from students. Questions to ponder include *Who is doing the thinking here—the teacher or the students? Who is asking the questions—the teacher or the students? How much of this lesson or activity is about students doing rather than thinking? Has the teacher done all the work for the students ahead of time, so the lesson or activity is reduced to a figurative "fill-in-the-blanks"? Is the lesson or activity overly prescriptive, or does it allow students to make choices and decisions?*

It is worth noting that some lessons or activities are not intended to be rigorous but, rather, aim to achieve a different goal, such as reinforcing a skill or teaching vocabulary. If this is the intention, then it may be appropriate for the activity to be less rigorous and more straightforward.

Differentiation. This dimension, which wasn't part of the original rubric that appears in *How Teachers Can Turn Data into Action* (Venables, 2014), was added at the request of teachers using the rubric in the field. The differentiation dimension compels the PLC to be mindful of the need to differentiate instruction in almost every lesson. Scoring a potential lesson or activity against this dimension raises awareness of this important aspect of good lesson design. Questions to think about include *Could this lesson or activity be better differentiated? Where? How? Does it lend itself to tiered experiences for diverse students? Is there something about this particular lesson component that should be one-size-fits-all? If the activity scores low on this dimension, is it easily fixable?*

Time-benefit analysis. This dimension forces the team to assess the time investment required against the likely learning gains in using the activity or lesson component. Questions to consider include *Is the amount (and quality) of learning that is likely to result commensurate with the time required (e.g., number of class periods)? If not, and substantive learning is nevertheless likely, can the amount of time required be trimmed without compromising that learning?*

Connections. This dimension was added to encourage PLCs to consider the degree to which the activity or lesson component produces learning that is not isolated but, rather, connects to previous and subsequent learning as well as to subject areas outside the course curriculum. Questions to think about include *Does this activity or lesson component produce learning in isolation? Does it connect to other subject areas (e.g., a probability activity that uses voting as its context, or a social studies activity that has students write a letter to local politicians that dovetails with an English language arts standard on writing persuasive essays)?*

The Planning Protocol Rubric is not intended to be the be-all and end-all of evaluation tools for reviewing lesson components or activities. To be sure, other dimensions could be added—for example, "degree to which activity connects to real-world situations or phenomena." Instead, the protocol is intended to be a relatively quick way for teachers and teacher teams to assess the "worthiness" of a lesson or lesson component they are considering implementing in their classes. The discussion that it elicits among PLC members is worth every minute spent. Whether all teachers reach consensus on each dimension's score is unimportant; what *is* important is that they are discussing important matters centered on lesson design, and they are constructing community knowledge as they engage in these discussions. The immediate and long-term benefits are momentous. And in time, after a few applications of the rubric, teachers get quick at using it.

The following Fly on the Wall takes a look at how our 8th grade social studies PLC uses the Planning Protocol Rubric to score a potential instructional activity.

FLY ON THE WALL

The Scene:
Using the Planning
Protocol Rubric

What Happened

Angie and the other members of the 8th grade social studies PLC have evidence that students consistently score poorly on Strand 3 of the 8th grade social studies standards: Civics and Government.[1] At the last meeting, all members agreed to find one promising instructional activity aligned to the standards in Strand 3 to review at the current meeting.[2] After reviewing all the activities brought by team members, the team decides to take a closer look at the activity Angie has brought[3] and score it using the Planning Protocol Rubric.

The instructional activity centers on a fairly elaborate voting simulation that students would participate in, complete with primary elections, third-party candidates, attack ads, gerrymandering, and members of the press (played by students). Teams of students would be required to write and submit persuasive speeches, an English language arts substandard. The activity has strong connections to math standards, including probability (predicting outcomes), graphing, and statistics. In addition, the unit incorporates several elements of the social studies economics strand, as teams are required to submit itemized budgets for advertising, travel for rallies, and other activities. Students can also raise money for their candidates.

After the members of the PLC quietly and individually score the unit along the dimensions of the Planning Protocol Rubric, they are ready to discuss the results.

Angie: OK, let's discuss how we scored this. We'll take one dimension of the rubric at a time, let everyone share the score they gave it and why, and have a brief discussion for each dimension. Remember, the goal is not to reach a consensus about a final score but, rather, to have useful conversations about what these dimensions mean and how they apply (or don't apply) to this unit.[4]

With that, team members share their scores and their rationales for those scores[5] and discuss the rubric dimensions, answering questions like *What does it mean for an activity to be engaging for students? How do we predict an activity's impact on student learning? What opportunities does this activity offer to embed technology?*[6] For each dimension, Angie shares her score last. This sends the message that her opinion is no more important or valid than anyone else's and that she values their opinions even above her own. There are many times when two or more teachers revel in agreement and a few times when teachers openly disagree[7] with each other. Angie does a little refereeing here and there but, for the most part, stays out of the disagreements as long as the participants remain respectful and the climate safe.[8]

During the scoring discussions, teachers make some suggestions to add, delete, or change some aspect of the unit to strengthen it along a particular dimension. Angie is careful to permit these suggestions without letting them take over the scoring discussion. She asks Evelyn to record the suggestions to refer to later.

After the team finishes discussing the last rubric dimension, Angie asks the capstone question of the meeting: *So, do we want to try this in our classes?* The team mulls over the question for seven or eight minutes and arrives at the answer *Yes, but with a few changes.* Angie then leads a team discussion of the merits of the suggestions that Evelyn has recorded.

(continued)

When there are only five minutes left of the meeting, Angie interrupts the discussion of suggestions, which is still going strong:

Angie: Let's hit the pause button here and debrief the process and decide next steps for continuing this.

The team obliges.

What's Worth Noting

[1]The team is responding to an evidence-based student learning gap, presumably one that is common to all the teachers' classes.

[2]It is important that each activity be new to the team and not something anyone has tried in the past. This reduces the personal stake each teacher has in the activity he or she has selected.

[3]There is insufficient time to examine and score all five activities the team has brought. By selecting what they believe is the most promising activity, team members are stacking the deck in favor of usability in the classroom.

[4]It is a good idea to remind team members of this goal, or else they can get bogged down and hyper-focused on the score rather than on constructing a shared understanding of each rubric dimension. The former pursuit has absolutely no effect on the future, whereas the latter will inform any future discussions that touch on those rubric dimensions.

[5]The remarkable degree of equity in PLC members' contributions during this process stands in stark contrast to customary teacher discussions. This leveled playing field encourages all members to contribute and reminds more vocal members to watch their airtime.

[6]This is constructing community knowledge at its finest. By sharing this experience in real time, the team is developing its own understanding of the characteristics of the dimensions. This understanding will be pivotal in future conversations and other team pursuits.

[7]Establishing that it's OK to openly disagree and to discuss those disagreements helps strengthen the team and its culture of safety by increasing levels of trust and risk taking.

[8]Here is where paying acute attention to nonverbal language is essential. Angie is "listening" not only to what is being said (and in what tone) but also to what is being communicated without actually being spoken aloud.

The Planning Protocol Rubric for Looking at Teacher Work

The Planning Protocol Rubric is well suited to vetting instructional methods and activities we are considering for use in the classroom. In this context, the methods or activities we are reviewing typically derive from outside sources—most often, lessons or lesson components we find on the Internet. The rubric is ideal for sifting through the disparate mass of activities available and homing in on the ones that pass muster according to the dimensions of the rubric. This use of the Planning Protocol Rubric generally occurs when the PLC collaboratively plans and implements lessons common to all teachers (or some subset of teachers) of a given subject or grade level.

In cases where the members of the PLC are not necessarily teaching the same grade or subject (for example, an Algebra PLC containing teachers of Algebra 1, Algebra 2, and Honors Algebra 1), a teacher might bring a lesson or an activity that he or she has designed to be vetted by the team using the Planning Protocol Rubric. This is a perfectly appropriate use of the rubric that every teacher in the PLC stands to gain from—not just the teacher whose work is being reviewed. In this way, the Planning Protocol Rubric can be used alongside other protocols for looking at teacher work, including the Notice and Wonder Protocol and the Tuning Protocol. A word of caution is in order, however: of these three tools for looking at teacher work, the Planning Protocol Rubric is the harshest on the presenting teacher in that it *scores* her work. Here's a ranking of the three review processes from "softest" to "harshest":

- Softest: Noticing and wondering about the work (Notice and Wonder Protocol)
- Medium: "Tuning the work" with warm and cool feedback (Tuning Protocol)
- Harshest: Scoring the work across multiple dimensions (Planning Protocol Rubric)

Unless the presenting teacher specifically requests the Planning Protocol Rubric for reviewing her work, there is a significant risk of defensiveness on her part resulting from its use. Therefore, I would suggest *not* using this tool for looking at a colleague's work until the team has used the Notice and Wonder Protocol and the Tuning Protocol with other work. There is a vast psychological difference between scoring a stranger's work found on the Internet and scoring a colleague's work. When the creator of the work is present during the scoring discussion, participants tend to temper comments, sidestep uncomfortable issues, and show much greater leniency than they would when scoring the work of an anonymous author. And although the safety of the presenting teacher is always paramount, we don't want candy-coated scores and comments that would afford no significant gain in the work.

The Charrette Protocol

The Charrette Protocol, which originated with and is still used in the architectural community, is used when a team encounters an obstacle in a design that is not yet finished. The protocol is a troubleshooting tool that brings the team together to problem-solve, which enables the work to be completed.

The Charrette Protocol is well suited for application to lessons, alternative assessments, project-based assignments, or other unit designs—particularly when one or two teachers on the team (as opposed to the entire team) are creating it and planning implementation. As with other protocols used to help a teacher's work improve or, in this case, move forward, the team's discussions directly benefit the presenting teacher(s) and indirectly benefit all the teachers on the team who have similar work or who face similar obstacles in their work. The protocol is sufficiently focused as to require only 30–35 minutes. The steps of the Charrette Protocol are outlined in Figure 10.2.

FIGURE 10.2 | Charrette Protocol

Purpose: Individual or multiple team members call for a Charrette when they are "stuck"—when they have reached a point in the process where they cannot easily move forward on their own.

Time: 30–35 minutes

Roles: Facilitator, presenting teacher(s), timekeeper

 I. The presenting teacher introduces and provides context for his or her "work in progress" and describes areas that need help while the rest of the team listens and takes notes. (5 minutes)

 II. The team asks clarifying questions of the presenting teacher. These questions are fact-finding; their purpose is to elicit additional relevant background information. Answers to clarifying questions are brief. (5 minutes)

 III. The team discusses the work while the presenting teacher listens and takes notes. The emphasis is on removing the stumbling block and improving the work, which now belongs to the entire group. The atmosphere is one of "we're in this together," and the work and solutions are referred to in ownership terms such as "we" and "our." Facilitators capitalize on and pursue fruitful lines of solutions by asking follow-up questions. (10–15 minutes)

 IV. When the presenting teacher believes he or she has gotten what was needed from the team, he or she stops the process and briefly reflects aloud on what was gained and what he or she believes the next steps are. The rest of the team is silent during this summary. (5 minutes)

 V. The team debriefs the process. (5 minutes)

Source: Special permission has been received to adapt the Charrette Protocol from the National School Reform Faculty. See http://www. nsrfharmony.org or call 812-330-2702 for other versions of the Charrette Protocol and to learn about coaches' training to use NSRF resources most effectively.

(Note: Although much of the content in this protocol comes from the National School Reform Faculty, this is a different Charrette Protocol than the one currently taught by the NSRF.)

The Charrette Protocol is similar to the Consultancy Protocol in that both revolve around some dilemma or issue that requires troubleshooting. The primary difference between the two is that the Charrette Protocol is ideal for issues that arise in the *design* of teacher work, whereas the Consultancy Protocol is better for issues that arise in the *implementation* or practice of teacher work. The Charrette is for obstacles born of content, while the Consultancy is for obstacles born of relationships. Further, the Charrette Protocol is designed to solicit PLC help for the teacher work *before* it is a finished product. The protocol helps reduce or eliminate obstacles along the way to completion. As in most work with authentic PLCs, there is always a gray area, and it is the facilitator's job to help the presenting teacher determine the best protocol for the obstacle or dilemma at hand.

When applied as prescribed, the Charrette Protocol fosters genuine collaboration among PLC members. Once the obstacle is identified, the entire PLC takes it on as its own—all the way to solution. This joint ownership of the presenting teacher's work distinguishes the Charrette from other protocols for looking at teacher work.

Planning for Improvement

Teachers spend a great deal of time planning. Any structure or tool for having high-level conversations about deciding which experiences we put our students through, what our target learning goals are, and how we ensure success in reaching those goals is worth routinely using. These tools force us to reflect on what could work, what has not worked, what needs tweaking, what needs scrapping, and what is worth keeping for next year. And rare as it can be, reflection on our practice may well be the most consequential catalyst to improvement that we have.

APPENDIX OF PROTOCOLS AND TOOLS

Irks and Quirks Protocol*

Time: 15 minutes

I. Each participant receives an index card. On one side of the card, participants write *one* pet peeve they have regarding working in groups or at teacher meetings. They begin their pet peeve with the phrase *It burns my butt when . . . .* (e.g., "It burns my butt when people come late to meetings," "It burns my butt when people are interrupted during discussions," or "It burns my butt when one person does all the talking."). (3 minutes)

II. On the other side of the card, participants write *one* trait about themselves that everyone in the group should know to best work with them in a group setting. They begin their trait with the phrase *One thing you all should know about me is . . . .* (e.g., "One thing you all should know about me is that my silence is not due to disinterest; I just need processing time," "One thing you all should know about me is I get excited during discussions, and sometimes people are put off by my enthusiasm," or "One thing you all should know about me is I am very visual and need to see what we're discussing on chart paper or the interactive whiteboard."). (3 minutes)

III. Participants share both sides of their cards in volunteer order **without discussion** (or elaborating on the card). (5 minutes)

IV. *The debrief.* The team members reflect aloud on the experience they have just shared. (4 minutes)

*Originally titled "Peeves and Traits" until Grapple participant Justine Szymala came up with this better name.

Source: Irks and Quirks is a pre-activity for setting up norms in teacher groups developed by Daniel R. Venables. From D. Venables, *The Practice of Authentic PLCs: A Guide to Effective Teacher Teams,* Corwin, 2011. Copyright 2011 by Corwin. Adapted with permission.

PLC Coach's Guide to Asking Deeper Questions

The role of the PLC coach or facilitator involves much more than simply delineating the agenda or leading PLC members through the steps of a timely protocol. Although these tasks have their place and are part of the PLC coach's "job description," they do not actually lead the PLC to do work that has a significant effect on student learning. To truly improve the work of the collective PLC and of individual teachers, PLC coaches must make a habit of asking probing, difficult questions.

Without addressing deeper questions, the team is just a group of teachers who go through a series of motions that have been approved as proper practices of a PLC, but who do nothing to improve student learning. The last thing busy teachers need is to participate in meetings that, in the end, do nothing of real or significant value to foster their students' learning.

I developed this guide, which draws from resources from the National School Reform Faculty's "Pocket Guide to Probing Questions," to help PLC coaches go deeper and push their PLC members to go deeper, so that they can make significant strides in instructional improvement. If PLCs are to do authentic, substantive work, PLC coaches must not only ask deeper questions and prompt PLC members to think on a deeper level but also relentlessly pursue asking these deeper questions. In my experience, this does not happen unless the PLC coach is aware of the importance of asking deeper questions and knows what such questions might look like.

Deeper questions . . .

- Are general and widely useful, often transcending the content of the moment.
- Allow for multiple responses.
- Help create a paradigm shift in the thinking of individuals and teams.
- Empower individuals and teams to think more expansively about a topic, an issue, or a dilemma.
- Avoid yes or no responses.
- Elicit slow, thoughtful responses.
- Move thinking from reaction to reflection, from being reactive to being proactive.
- Encourage taking another party's perspective.

Some questions that help push data conversations include the following:

- What do you think that implies?
- Do you think we have evidence to support that statement? Where?
- Can you point to specific evidence?
- Why? How do you know?
- Do you think this is something that is systemic or specific to particular student populations?

- What do you think we should do to address that?
- What are the big issues here, as opposed to the secondary or ancillary issues?
- Can we see root causes, based on the evidence, that give rise to secondary symptoms in the issues we're seeing? What are the root causes?

Some general question stems that help push deeper thinking include the following:

- Why do you think this is the case?
- What would have to change in order for . . . ?
- What do you feel is right in your gut?
- What do you wish . . . ?
- What's another way you might . . . ?
- What would it look like if . . . ?
- What do you think would happen if . . . ?
- How was [*ABC*] different from [*XYZ*]?
- What sort of effect do you think [*ABC*] would have on [*XYZ*]?
- What criteria did you use to . . . ?
- When have you done/experienced something like this before?
- What might you see happening in your classroom if . . . ?
- How did you determine that [*XYZ*] was best?
- What is your hunch about . . . ?
- What was your intention when . . . ?
- What do you assume to be true about . . . ?
- What is the connection between [*ABC*] and [*XYZ*]?
- What if the opposite were true? What would happen?
- How might your assumptions about [*ABC*] have influenced how you were thinking about [*XYZ*]?
- Why is this such a dilemma for you?

When team members address deeper questions, important truths about instructional practice come to light. It's not that teachers have been hiding anything; it's more that they have not spent adequate time really looking at what they do and, more important, at the effect of their actions on student learning. It is the PLC coach's job to push this kind of questioning so that these truths bubble to the surface during discourse. The questions and question stems in this guide can help.

Source: Developed by D. R. Venables, Center for Authentic PLCs (www.authenticplcs.com), drawing from resources from NSRF's "Pocket Guide to Probing Questions." Special permission has been received to reproduce text from the National School Reform Faculty. See http://www.nsrfharmony.org or call 812-330-2702 for more resources and to learn about coaches' training to use NSRF resources most effectively.

Text-Based Seminar Guidelines

Purpose: To enlarge understanding of a text (not achieve some particular understanding)

Ground Rules:

1. Listen actively.
2. Build on what others say.
3. Don't step on others' talk. Silences and pauses are OK.
4. Let the conversation flow as much as possible without raising hands or using a speaker's list.
5. Make the assumptions underlying your comments explicit to others.
6. Emphasize clarification, amplification, and implications of ideas.
7. Watch your own airtime—both in terms of how often you speak and in terms of how much you say when you speak.
8. Refer to the text; challenge others to go to the text.

Source: NSRF. Special permission has been received to reproduce the Text-Based Seminar from the National School Reform Faculty. See http://www.nsrfharmony.org or call 812-330-2702 for more resources and to learn about coaches' training to use NSRF resources most effectively.

Final Word Protocol

Time: 55 minutes

I. Team members individually highlight or annotate the common text that they have already read. Each person selects one or two significant quotes or sections from the text. Each excerpt should consist of at least a sentence but be no longer than a short paragraph. (6 minutes)

II. Participants work in groups of four*, with a designated timekeeper, facilitator, and first speaker for each round. The facilitator's role is to ensure that the group stays focused, while the timekeeper's role is to make sure that participants stick to the times. There are four rounds of 11 minutes each (44 minutes total). Here's what each round looks like:

1. The first speaker reads one of his or her selections from the text and then explains the significance of the excerpt and why he or she chose it. *Others in the group are not permitted to speak during this time.* (3 minutes)

2. Each participant, in turn, gets 2 minutes to comment on the first speaker's selection. Team members may choose to respond to what the first speaker has said *or* to speak to the excerpt itself in any way that extends the group's understanding of the text. No one is permitted to speak except the person whose turn it is to speak. (6 minutes)

3. After his or her fellow team members have spoken, the first speaker has the **FINAL WORD**. (2 minutes)

Rounds 2, 3, and 4 begin by rotating the roles of first speaker, facilitator, and timekeeper.

III. The team debriefs the process. (5 minutes)

*Groups of five or six are also appropriate, although their rounds would require 65 and 90 minutes, respectively. Each round can be trimmed, if necessary. Divide a team with seven members into two groups, one of three and one of four, with the recognition that the larger group will finish after the smaller group. If time is limited, a team of six can also be split into two groups of three.

Source: NSRF. Special permission has been received to reproduce the Final Word Protocol from the National School Reform Faculty. See http://www.nsrfharmony.org or call 812-330-2702 for more resources and to learn about coaches' training to use NSRF resources most effectively.

Essential Highlights Protocol

Time: 30 minutes

Purpose: To collaboratively construct meaning from, clarify, and expand thinking about a text

Materials: Hard copies of the text to be discussed and highlighters in yellow, blue, and pink

Setup: Participants sit in a circle or around a conference table.

Roles: Facilitator, timekeeper

  I. *Round 1:* Team members individually read and highlight the text as they normally would, using the *yellow* highlighter. Each then passes his or her highlighted copy of the text to his or her left-hand neighbor. (5 minutes)

 II. *Round 2:* Team members individually read the highlighted portions of the text they have received from their neighbor and highlight in *blue* a single yellow-highlighted sentence from each yellow-highlighted excerpt in the text. No new sentences may be highlighted—only those previously highlighted in *yellow*. Each team member then passes his or her double-highlighted copy of the text to his or her left-hand neighbor. (5 minutes)

III. *Round 3:* Team members individually read the highlighted portions of the text they have received and highlight in *pink* a single phrase from each highlighted excerpt in the text. No new phrases may be highlighted—only those previously highlighted in *yellow* or in *yellow and blue*. Each team member then returns the text to its original owner. (5 minutes)

 IV. Team members take turns sharing with the group the *pink*-highlighted phrases from their original copies of the text. (5 minutes)

  V. The team discusses any new insights about the text that may have emerged. (5 minutes)

 VI. The team debriefs the process. (5 minutes)

Source: Developed by D. R. Venables, Center for Authentic PLCs (www.authenticplcs.com).

Notice and Wonder Protocol for Student Work

Time: 40 minutes

Roles: Facilitator, timekeeper, presenting teacher

Purpose: To analyze student work

I. *The context.* (5 minutes)
   - The presenting teacher gives the context for the work he or she has volunteered to share. Other team members are silent and take notes. (2 minutes)
   - The presenting teacher distributes relevant documents for the team to review. (3 minutes)

II. *Clarifying questions.* The team asks clarifying questions of the presenter. These questions should be free of judgment; their sole aim is to elicit additional information. Answers to these questions are short, often a single statement. (5 minutes)

III. Quietly and individually, participants write three or four Notice Statements based on their observations of the work. These statements, which begin with the phrase "I notice that . . . ," must be free of inference, judgment, or speculation; they are fact-based, observing only what is already present in the work. (3 minutes)

IV. *Round 1: Notice Statements.* Team members take turns reading aloud one new Notice Statement at a time, *without discussion,* while the presenting teacher quietly takes notes. The process continues until all Notice Statements have been shared. (4 minutes)

V. Quietly and individually, participants write three or four Wonder Statements about the work. These statements, which begin with the phrase "I wonder why/if/how/whether . . . ," may or may not relate directly to Notice Statements shared in Round 1. Sometimes they offer a suggestion; other times they are merely inquiries to help the presenting teacher think more expansively about his or her work. (5 minutes)

VI. *Round 2: Wonder Statements.* In no particular order, team members take turns reading aloud one new Wonder Statement at a time while the presenting teacher quietly takes notes. This process continues until all Wonder Statements have been shared, *without discussion, except* in cases where the facilitator chooses to ask follow-up questions of a teacher sharing a Wonder Statement or of the whole team. (8 minutes)

VII. *Teacher reflection.* The presenting teacher takes a moment to review his or her notes and then reflects aloud on any or all of the comments made by the team. The rest of the team is silent. (5 minutes)

VIII. *The debrief.* The team members debrief the experience they have just shared. (5 minutes)

Source: The Notice and Wonder Protocol for Student Work (v2.0) is a protocol for looking at student work developed by Daniel R. Venables. From D. Venables, *The Practice of Authentic PLCs: A Guide to Effective Teacher Teams,* Corwin, 2011. Copyright 2011 by Corwin. Adapted with permission.

Notice, Like, and Wonder Protocol for Teacher Work

Time: 50 minutes

Roles: Facilitator, timekeeper, presenting teacher

Purpose: Improving a teacher's (or teachers') work

I. *The context.* (5 minutes)
   - The presenting teacher gives the context for the work he or she has volunteered to share. Other team members are silent and take notes. (2 minutes)
   - The presenting teacher distributes relevant documents for the team to review. (3 minutes)

II. *Clarifying questions.* The team asks clarifying questions of the presenter. These questions should be free of judgment; their sole aim is to elicit additional information. Answers to these questions are short, often a single statement. (5 minutes)

III. Quietly and individually, participants write three or four Notice Statements based on their observations of the work. These statements, which begin with the phrase "I notice that . . . ," must be free of inference, judgment, or speculation; they are fact-based, observing only what is already present in the work. (3 minutes)

IV. *Round 1: Notice Statements.* Team members take turns reading aloud one new Notice Statement at a time, *without discussion,* while the presenting teacher quietly takes notes. The process continues until all Notice Statements have been shared. (4 minutes)

V. Quietly and individually, participants write three or four Like Statements based on their observations of the work. These statements, which begin with the phrase "I like . . . ," are based on personal preferences. (3 minutes)

VI. *Round 2: Like Statements.* Team members take turns reading aloud one new Like Statement at a time, *without discussion,* while the presenting teacher quietly takes notes. The process continues until all Like Statements have been shared. (5 minutes)

VII. Quietly and individually, participants write three or four Wonder Statements about the work. These statements, which begin with the phrase "I wonder why/

if/how/whether . . . ," may or may not relate directly to Notice Statements shared in Round 1. Sometimes they offer a suggestion; other times they are merely inquiries to help the presenting teacher think more expansively about his or her work. (5 minutes)

VIII. *Round 3: Wonder Statements.* In no particular order, team members take turns reading aloud one new Wonder Statement at a time while the presenting teacher quietly takes notes. This process continues until all Wonder Statements have been shared, *without discussion, except* in cases where the facilitator chooses to ask follow-up questions of a teacher sharing a Wonder Statement or of the whole team. (10 minutes)

IX. *Teacher reflection.* The presenting teacher takes a moment to review his or her notes and then reflects aloud on any or all of the comments made by the team. The rest of the team is silent. (5 minutes)

X. *The debrief.* The team members debrief the experience they have just shared. (5 minutes)

Source: The Notice, Like, and Wonder Protocol for Teacher Work is a protocol for looking at teacher work developed by Daniel R. Venables. From D. Venables, *The Practice of Authentic PLCs: A Guide to Effective Teacher Teams,* Corwin, 2011. Copyright 2011 by Corwin. Adapted with permission. This version includes contributions from the fine folks at Caldwell-West Caldwell Schools.

Tuning Protocol for Looking at Teacher Work

Time: 40 minutes

Roles: Facilitator, timekeeper, presenting teacher(s)

Purpose: Improving a teacher's (or teachers') work

I. *Presentation of work.* (5 minutes)
 - The presenting teacher discusses the context for the work he or she has volunteered to share, including goals (teacher and student), whether he or she has already used the work with students or is planning to use the work, relevant information about the students or topic, and an area of focus for the feedback, if there is one. Other team members are silent and take notes. (3 minutes)
 - The presenting teacher distributes handouts or supporting documents for the team to review. (2 minutes)

II. *Clarifying questions.* As participants review the handouts, they may ask clarifying questions of the presenter. These questions are fact-based (e.g., who, what, when, how long) and should be nonevaluative; their sole aim is to elicit additional information. The presenting teacher answers these questions in brief statements. (5 minutes)

III. *Participant reflection.* Participants continue to review the work and collect their thoughts about feedback they will share in segment IV. There is no discussion during this time. (5 minutes)

IV. *Feedback.* Participants talk with one another about the work, referring to the presenting teacher in the third person (if at all), while the presenting teacher quietly takes notes. The group begins with *warm* feedback (3–5 minutes) and then moves on to *cool* feedback, which may or may not be accompanied by suggestions (10 minutes). The facilitator may ask occasional follow-up questions to participants during the discussion. (15 minutes)

V. *Teacher reflection.* The presenting teacher takes a moment to review his or her notes and then reflects aloud on any items he or she chooses. The rest of the team listens without discussion. (5 minutes)

VI. *The debrief.* The facilitator leads a discussion about the experience. (5 minutes)

Source: Adapted by D. R. Venables from McDonald's Tuning Protocol. Please note that this is not the NSRF Tuning Protocol, although other instances of NSRF protocols appear in this book.

Facilitating Teacher Teams and Authentic PLCs: The Human Side of Leading People, Protocols, and Practices by Daniel R. Venables. © 2018 ASCD.

Notice and Wonder Protocol for Data (v2.0)

Time: 40 minutes

Roles: Facilitator, timekeeper, scribe

Purpose: To look descriptively and inferentially at data

I. Participants are presented with a graph or table of data pertaining to their practice. The data may be displayed on a screen for all to see, or they may be given to each PLC member in hard-copy format. (The former is preferable, since graphs and tables of data are often illustrated in color.)

II. Quietly and individually, participants write three or four Notice Statements based on their observations of the graph or table of data. These statements, which begin with the phrase "I notice that . . . ," must be free of inference, judgment, or speculation; they are factual, based on objective examination of the display, and reflect only what is present in the data. (5 minutes)

III. *Round 1: Notice Statements.* Team members take turns reading aloud one new Notice Statement at a time, *without discussion*. The process continues until all Notice Statements have been shared. (5 minutes)

IV. Quietly and individually, participants write three or four Wonder Statements or question-statements about the data. These statements, which begin with the phrase "I wonder why/if/how/whether . . . ," may or may not relate directly to Notice Statements shared in Round 1. Their intent is to gain insight into what the data suggest, how the data are connected, and what the data imply. (5 minutes)

V. *Round 2: Wonder Statements.* Team members take turns reading aloud one new Wonder Statement at a time while the scribe records the statements on chart paper or types them into a document. This process continues until all Wonder Statements have been shared, *without discussion, except* in cases where the facilitator chooses to ask follow-up questions of a teacher sharing a Wonder Statement or of the whole team. (10 minutes)

VI. *The debrief: Content.* The PLC discusses the data and the statements that have been shared, including possible root causes and connections to classroom instruction, and takes note of additional data that may be needed to gain further insight. (10 minutes)

VII. *The debrief: Process.* The team debriefs the process it has just experienced. (5 minutes)

Potential Data Discussion Pitfalls*:
How Would You Handle Them?

* aka *Opportunities*

Time: 35 minutes

    I. Participants pair off (*A, B*) and access a virtual 10-sided die (e.g., by download-ing a dice-rolling app like Dice Roller or The Game Dice Roller or visiting http://www.roll-dice-online.com).

  II. *Rounds.* (10 minutes each, 20 minutes total)

      1. Participant *A* rolls the virtual decahedron die to determine which pitfall of the 10 listed in the table below he or she will troubleshoot. Participant *A* has five minutes to collect his or her thoughts *and* share with Participant *B* how he or she would respond. Participant *B* keeps track of the time and does not speak.

      2. Participant *B* has two minutes to respond to Participant *A*'s solution. Participant *A* keeps track of the time and does not speak.

      3. Participants *A* and *B* have three minutes to articulate in the table their best collective thinking on how to address the pitfall.

      4. Participants repeat steps 1–3, this time switching roles, and rolling again if they get the same pitfall as the first time.

  III. *Discussion.* Pairs return to the table and share their pitfalls and solutions with other pairs. (10 minutes)

  IV. *Large-group debrief.* (5 minutes)

Pitfall	What would you ask, say, or do?
1. Focus of data conversation shifts to issues over which the team has no control.	
2. Focus of data conversation is on trivial, relatively unimportant observations.	

Pitfall	What would you ask, say, or do?
3. The team is quick to blame students and reluctant to accept responsibility for learning gaps.	
4. Data conversation becomes micro-focused on one particular student or test item.	
5. Focus of data conversation shifts to skills students "should have acquired before this year."	
6. Team jumps prematurely to proposing solutions.	
7. Focus of data conversation shifts to items unrelated to the data at hand.	
8. Focus of data conversation is on secondary symptoms of an undiscussed primary issue.	
9. Team is celebratory and self-congratulatory about what is working.	
10. Focus of data conversation shifts to sustained sentiments of helplessness and pessimism.	

Consultancy Protocol

Purpose: To open up people's minds to new ways of thinking about a problem or issue related to teaching and learning

Roles: Facilitator, presenting teacher(s), timekeeper

Pre-work for the Presenting Teacher: Writing About the Dilemma

Consider the dilemma. The dilemma should be an issue with which you are struggling, that has a way to go before being resolved, that is up to you to control, and that is crucial to your work. It is important that your problem be authentic and fresh—that is, not already solved or nearly solved.

Write a short paragraph summarizing the dilemma. Use the following questions to guide your writing:

1. Why is this a dilemma for you? Why is this dilemma important to you?
2. If you could take a snapshot of this dilemma, what would you/we see?
3. What have you already done to try to remedy or manage the dilemma?
4. What have been the results of those attempts?
5. Who do you hope changes? Who do you hope will take action to resolve this dilemma? If your answer is not *you,* you need to change your focus. The dilemma you present should be about *your* practice, behaviors, beliefs, and assumptions, not someone else's.
6. What do you assume to be true about this dilemma? How have these assumptions influenced your thinking about the dilemma?

The Consultancy Protocol

Time: 40 minutes

I. *Presenter overview.* The presenter gives an overview of the dilemma for the team to consider. (3 minutes)

II. *Clarifying questions.* (5 minutes)
- Participants ask clarifying questions of the presenter. Clarifying questions can be answered with facts.
- If the questions are not clarifying, they should be rephrased so that they are or saved for the subsequent participant discussion.

III. *Probing questions.* (7 minutes)
- Participants ask probing questions of the presenter. The purpose of probing questions is to expand the presenter's thinking about the issue to jump-start analysis of the dilemma.

- The presenter may choose not to respond to a question by saying, "Pass on that one" or "Let me think about that."

IV. *Participant discussion.* (15 minutes)
- The presenter withdraws from the group, taking notes on the participants' discussion of the dilemma. Participants talk with one another without addressing the presenter.
- Participants may describe actions that the presenter could take, but they should not feel as though they need to arrive at a solution to the dilemma.
- Suggested questions for the facilitator to ask to get the discussion going include
  - What did we hear?
  - What didn't we hear that we think might be relevant?
  - What assumptions seem to be operating?
  - What questions does the dilemma raise for us?
  - What do we think about the dilemma?
  - What might we do or try if faced with a similar dilemma? What have we done in similar situations?

V. *Presenter reflection.* (5 minutes)
- Referring to notes taken during the participant discussion, the presenter reflects on the participants' comments and their effect on his or her thinking.
- It is particularly important for the presenter to share new insights that the discussion has provided.

VI. *Debrief.* The facilitator leads the group in a discussion of the protocol process. (5 minutes)

Source: This protocol was developed in conjunction with the Coalition of Essential Schools and the Annenberg Institute for School Reform, which became the National School Reform Faculty. The NSRF now recommends one or more variations on this protocol. Special permission has been received to reproduce the Consultancy Protocol from NSRF. See http://www.nsrfharmony.org or call 812-330-2702 for more resources and to learn about coaches' training to use NSRF resources most effectively.

Shared Dilemma Protocol (v2.0)

Purpose: Teacher teams often experience dilemmas or problems that are pervasive across a grade level or subject area. This protocol provides a structured way for teacher teams to start the process of solving a shared dilemma or problem that is within their sphere of influence or control.

Time: 45 minutes

Roles: Facilitator (explains each step, moderates, and participates), timekeeper, recorder

Pre-work: A specific dilemma that most members of the PLC face is identified in a prior meeting

   I. *The dilemma.* The facilitator presents the common dilemma to the group. Participants may ask a few clarifying questions to ensure that everyone has necessary information. (3 minutes)

  II. *Probing questions.* (17 minutes)
    1. Participants are given five minutes to quietly write one probing question that will encourage deeper conversation about the dilemma. During the next two minutes, participants take turns sharing their questions without discussion while the recorder writes them on chart paper or a whiteboard or in a digital format that everyone can see. (7 minutes)
    2. Participants take time to respond to and discuss some or all of the probing questions on the list. The recorder writes the responses on chart paper or a whiteboard or in a digital format. (10 minutes)

 III. *Solutions.* (10 minutes)
    1. Participants brainstorm possible solutions. Again, the recorder writes the ideas where everyone can see them. (5 minutes)
    2. Participants engage in an open discussion about the proposed solutions and are encouraged to ask clarifying questions to gain a better understanding of these possible solutions. (5 minutes)

  IV. *Next steps.* The facilitator asks questions like "What will we do now based on this discussion? Which solutions should we put into an action plan? Which solutions should we investigate further? Which solutions are we ready to agree to implement?" The recorder takes notes using the chart below to organize ideas. (10 minutes)

	Description	Timeline	Responsible Party
Solutions requiring investigation			
Solutions to put into action			

V.   *Debrief.* (5 minutes)

Source: Protocol first developed by Cari Begin with contributions from Daniel R. Venables to help teacher teams start the process of solving a shared dilemma over which they have control. © 2013 by Cari Begin. Revised by Daniel R. Venables © 2016.

Planning Protocol Rubric (v3.0)

Dimension	1	2	3	4
Alignment to Standards	Barely aligned or not aligned	Somewhat aligned	Mostly aligned	Completely aligned
Impact on Learning	Low impact	Medium-low impact	Medium-high impact	High impact
Student Engagement	Low engagement for most students	Moderate engagement for some students	Moderate engagement for most students	High engagement for most students
Depth of Knowledge Level	Recall	Skill/concept	Strategic reasoning	Extended reasoning
Technology Integration	No integration of technology	Some integration of technology	Effective and prominent integration of technology	Effective and innovative integration of technology
Teacher Friendliness		High-maintenance (lots of materials and prep work)	Low-maintenance (few materials or little prep work)	
Rigor and Relevance	Teacher works	Students work	Students think	Students think and work
Differentiation	Not suited for differentiation	Suited for differentiation with fairly significant modifications	Well suited for differentiation with minor modifications	Well suited for differentiation as is, with natural tiers built in
Time-Benefit Analysis	Too much instructional time required for relatively little learning	Questionable amount of time required for expected amount of learning	Amount of time required and amount of learning are commensurate	Small amount of time required for amount of learning that exceeds expectations

Dimension	1	2	3	4
Connections	No connections to previous or future standards or to other subjects	A few genuine connections to other standards or subjects	Genuine connections to other standards and/or subjects embedded in various components	Strong, authentic connections to previous and future standards and to other subjects

Copyright 2013–2017 by Daniel R. Venables.

Charrette Protocol

Purpose: Individual or multiple team members call for a Charrette when they are "stuck"—when they have reached a point in the process where they cannot easily move forward on their own.

Time: 30–35 minutes

Roles: Facilitator, presenting teacher(s), timekeeper

I. The presenting teacher introduces and provides context for his or her "work in progress" and describes areas that need help while the rest of the team listens and takes notes. (5 minutes)

II. The team asks clarifying questions of the presenting teacher. These questions are fact-finding; their purpose is to elicit additional relevant background information. Answers to clarifying questions are brief. (5 minutes)

III. The team discusses the work while the presenting teacher listens and takes notes. The emphasis is on removing the stumbling block and improving the work, which now belongs to the entire group. The atmosphere is one of "we're in this together," and the work and solutions are referred to in ownership terms such as "we" and "our." Facilitators capitalize on and pursue fruitful lines of solutions by asking follow-up questions. (10–15 minutes)

IV. When the presenting teacher believes he or she has gotten what was needed from the team, he or she stops the process and briefly reflects aloud on what was gained and what he or she believes the next steps are. The rest of the team is silent during this summary. (5 minutes)

V. The team debriefs the process. (5 minutes)

Source: Special permission has been received to adapt the Charrette Protocol from the National School Reform Faculty. See http://www.nsrfharmony.org or call 812-330-2702 for other versions of the Charrette Protocol and to learn about coaches' training to use NSRF resources most effectively.

The Mindful Debrief: A Pocket Guide to Debriefing

The Context

Reflection is an important practice of authentic PLCs. Just as teachers reflect on a lesson they've given to students or on test results from a recent assessment, PLCs reflect on the work they do—very often at the conclusion of a particular collaborative task. Such a reflection is called *the debrief* of whatever task the PLC has engaged in, and it is intended to provide a forum in which PLC members can discuss the process—what worked and what could be better next time. Debriefing encourages quicker growth in the PLC; protocols and processes that may have been awkward the first go-round become refined, efficient, and more productive in really making a difference in classroom instruction and student learning. Debriefing also allows reluctant PLC members to speak their minds about tasks in which the PLC has engaged. It is the perfect forum for lodging concerns and constructive criticism. PLCs that make a regular habit of mindfully debriefing stand to grow twice as fast as teams that never reflect on what they've done and what they're doing.

Questions to Consider

The following questions are meant to guide the PLC facilitator in debriefing. *Do not feel compelled to address them all;* these represent a sampling of the kinds of questions a facilitator might ask of her PLC during the debrief. *Remember:* the debrief is a time to reflect on the *process*—not on the particular content that was the focus of the activity/protocol.

- How did it go? Did you like this protocol?
- What worked well?
- What could we do better next time?
- What might we change for next time? How would that make it better?
- Did we rush the protocol?
- Did we go deep enough?
- Did we stay on task?
- Will our students benefit from our having done this? How?
- Have we experienced a growth spurt from the last time we engaged in this task [or a similar experience]? In what area?
- How often should we engage in this protocol/task/discussion? What makes sense?

How Did Our Facilitator Do?

Did the facilitator . . .

- Encourage all voices?
- Remind members to watch airtime, as needed?
- Keep team members focused?
- Redirect digressive conversations or comments, as needed?
- Preserve the safety of all team members during other members' contributions?
- Call team members on infractions of norms or protocol rules?
- Ask thought-encouraging questions?
- Ask rich follow-up questions, as appropriate?
- Offer a clear explanation of purpose and how the protocol worked?
- Restate directions for each segment, as needed?
- Follow protocol times and conclude the protocol at the appropriate stopping point?
- Lead the team in a meaningful debrief of process?

How Did We Do?

Did all PLC members . . .

- Seem actively engaged?
- Invest in the work?
- Maintain focus on the task?
- Follow the norms or protocol rules?
- Engage in rich (versus superficial) discussion?
- Offer honest but respectful contributions?

Comments?

BIBLIOGRAPHY

Allen, D., & Blythe, T. (2004). *The facilitator's book of questions: Tools for looking together at student and teacher work.* New York: Teachers College Press.

Begin, C. (2013). *Shared dilemma protocol.* Unpublished manuscript.

Blythe, T., Allen, D., & Powell, B. S. (2015). *Looking together at student work.* New York: Teachers College Press.

Chappuis, J. (2012). "How am I doing?" *Educational Leadership, 70*(1), 36–41.

Clark, S. B., & Duggins, A. S. (2016). *Using quality feedback to guide professional learning: A framework for instructional leaders.* Thousand Oaks, CA: Corwin.

Cloud, H., & Townsend, J. S. (2012). *Boundaries: When to say yes, how to say no to take control of your life.* Grand Rapids, MI: Zondervan Books.

Covey, S. R. (2014). *The 7 habits of highly effective people: Powerful lessons in personal change.* New York: Simon & Schuster.

Dewey, J. (1938/2015). *Experience and education.* New York: Free Press.

DuFour, R., DuFour, R., & Eaker, R. (2008). *Revisiting professional learning communities at work: New insights for improving schools.* Bloomington, IN: Solution Tree.

Dweck, C. S. (2006). *Mindset: The new psychology of success.* New York: Random House.

Evans, R. (2001). *The human side of school change: Reform, resistance, and the real-life problems of innovation.* San Francisco: Jossey-Bass.

Fullan, M. (2011). *Change leader: Learning to do what matters most.* Hoboken, NJ: Wiley.

Fullan, M. (2014). *Leading in a culture of change.* Hoboken, NJ: Wiley.

Fullan, M. (2016). *The new meaning of educational change.* New York: Teachers College Press.

Gladwell, M. (2000). *The tipping point: How little things can make a big difference.* New York: Little, Brown.

Hargreaves, A., & Fullan, M. (2012). *Professional capital: Transforming teaching in every school.* New York: Teachers College Press.

Leana, C. R. (2011, Fall). The missing link in school reform. *Stanford Social Innovation Review, 9*(4), 30–35. Available: https://ssir.org/articles/entry/the_missing_link_in_school_reform

Lencioni, P. (2005). *Overcoming the five dysfunctions of a team: A field guide for leaders, managers, and facilitators.* San Francisco: Jossey-Bass.

McDonald, J. P. (2013). *The power of protocols: An educator's guide to better practice.* New York: Teachers College Press.

National Governors Association for Best Practices (NGA Center) & Chief Council of State School Officers (CCSSO). (2010). *Common Core State Standards.* Washington, DC: Author.

National School Reform Faculty [NSRF]. (2000). *Resource book.* Bloomington, IN: Author.

NSRF. (n.d.). *Charrette protocol.* Bloomington, IN: Author.

NSRF. (n.d.). *Considerations for responsive facilitation.* Bloomington, IN: Author.

NSRF. (n.d.). *Consultancy protocol.* Bloomington, IN: Author.

NSRF. (n.d.). *Final word protocol.* Bloomington, IN: Author.

NSRF. (n.d.). *Four As protocol.* Bloomington, IN: Author.

NSRF. (n.d.). *Pocket guide to probing questions.* Bloomington, IN: Author.

NSRF. (n.d.). *Text-based seminar.* Bloomington, IN: Author.

NSRF. (n.d.). *Tuning protocol.* Bloomington, IN: Author.

Palmer, P. J. (2007). *The courage to teach: Exploring the inner landscape of a teacher's life.* San Francisco: Jossey-Bass/Wiley.

Reeves, D. B. (2009). *Leading change in your school: How to conquer myths, build commitment, and get results.* Alexandria, VA: ASCD.

Shanks, J., Beck, J., & Staloch, T. (2006). Westward expansion as a metaphor for educational change. *Journal of Research for Educational Leaders, 3*(2), 92–101. Retrieved from http://www2.education.uiowa.edu/archives/jrel/spring06/Shanks_0513.htm

Sizer, T. R. (2004). *Horace's compromise: The dilemma of the American high school.* Boston: Houghton Mifflin.

Stangor, C. (2011). *Principles of social psychology* (1st international ed.). Retrieved from https://opentextbc.ca/socialpsychology

Venables, D. R. (2011). *The practice of authentic PLCs: A guide to effective teacher teams.* Thousand Oaks, CA: Corwin.

Venables, D. R. (2014). *How teachers can turn data into action.* Alexandria, VA: ASCD.

Venables, D. R. (2015a, April). The case for protocols. *Educational Leadership, 72*(7). Retrieved from http://www.ascd.org/publications/educational-leadership/apr15/vol72/num07/The-Case-for-Protocols.aspx

Venables, D. R. (2015b). *The mindful debrief: A pocket guide to debriefing.* Unpublished manuscript.

Webb, N. L., Alt, M., Ely, R., & Vesperman, B. (2005, July 24). *Depth of knowledge web alignment tool.* Wisconsin Center for Educational Research. Madison, WI: University of Wisconsin. Retrieved from http://wat.wceruw.org/index.aspx

Weinberger, D. (2011). *Too big to know: Rethinking knowledge now that the facts aren't the facts, experts are everywhere, and the smartest person in the room is the room.* New York: Basic Books.

Wikipedia contributors. (2017). Navigator. *Wikipedia.* Retrieved from https://en.wikipedia.org/w/index.php?title=Navigator&oldid=788860464

INDEX

Note: Page references followed by an italicized *f* indicate information contained in figures.

ABOUT THE AUTHOR

Daniel R. Venables is an education consultant and the founding director of the Center for Authentic PLCs, an organization committed to assisting schools in building, leading, and sustaining authentic PLCs and doing well the important tasks in which authentic PLCs engage. Through the Center, he developed the *Grapple™ Institutes,* which have trained hundreds of teacher leaders to become highly effective PLC facilitators. He is the author of the national best-seller *How Teachers Can Turn Data into Action* (ASCD, 2014) and *The Practice of Authentic PLCs: A Guide to Effective Teacher Teams* (Corwin, 2011). He frequently presents at national conferences and writes as a guest blogger for national education blogs, including *TeachersCount* and *EdWeek.*

Mr. Venables's experience in education as an award-winning classroom teacher, a speaker and consultant, and a professional development coordinator with the United States' 18th-largest district, Charlotte-Mecklenburg Schools, spans more than 30 years. He has spent 24 years as a classroom teacher in both public and independent schools in South Carolina, North Carolina, and Connecticut, serving as a department chair for 18 of those years. In 2002 he was awarded South Carolina Independent School Teacher of the Year. As far back as 1993–1994, he was trained as a Math/Science Fellow with the Coalition of Essential Schools (CES), where he began his experience with Critical Friends Groups (CFGs) and their offspring, professional learning communities (PLCs). Since that time, he has assisted dozens of rural and urban schools throughout the United States in developing high-functioning teacher teams/PLCs. He speaks regularly at educational conferences across the country and in 2014 offered the keynote address at the Archdiocese of Detroit Educational Conference, where he learned that his books are required reading for Michigan State College of Education students. In 2014, Mr. Venables became a member of the ASCD National Professional Learning Faculty.

Mr. Venables's presentation style is energetic and humorous, and his message is practical, rooted in his experiences in the classroom and working with teachers. Whether presenting at national conferences or offering ongoing, site-based assistance to individual schools, he is always well received by teachers and administrators. At the heart of it, Mr. Venables cares deeply for kids, their teachers, and the work that authentic professional learning communities can do to make a real impact on how much and how many kids learn. He can be contacted at dvenables@authenticPLCs .com or at 803-206-3578, or on Twitter (@authenticplcs). Contact him if you would like information about bringing a Grapple Institute to your school or district.

Related ASCD Resources

At the time of publication, the following resources were available (ASCD stock numbers in parentheses).

PD Online® Courses

Leading Professional Learning: Building Capacity Through Teacher Leaders (#PD13OC010M)

Schools as Professional Learning Communities: An Introduction (#PD09OC28)

Print Products

The Artisan Teaching Model for Instructional Leadership: Working Together to Transform Your School by Kenneth Baum and David Krulwich (#116041)

How Teachers Can Turn Data into Action by Daniel R. Venables (#114007)

Protocols for Professional Learning (The Professional Learning Community Series) by Lois Brown Easton (#109037)

Strengthening and Enriching Your Professional Learning Community: The Art of Learning Together by Geoffrey Caine and Renate H. Caine (#110085)

Taking Charge of Professional Development: A Practical Model for Your School by Joseph H. Semadeni (#109029)

Teacher Teamwork: How do we make it work? (ASCD Arias) by Margaret Searle and Marilyn Swartz (#SF115045)

For up-to-date information about ASCD resources, go to www.ascd.org. You can search the complete archives of *Educational Leadership* at www.ascd.org/el.

Videos

The Reflective Educator: A Collaborative Approach to Building Teachers' Capacity DVD with Peter A. Hall and Alisa Simeral (#616027)

The Strategic Teacher DVD (#610137)

ASCD EDge® Group

Exchange ideas and connect with other educators on the social networking site ASCD EDge at http://ascdedge.ascd.org/

ASCD myTeachSource®

Download resources from a professional learning platform with hundreds of research-based best practices and tools for your classroom at http://myteachsource.ascd.org/

For more information, send an e-mail to member@ascd.org; call 1-800-933-2723 or 703-578-9600; send a fax to 703-575-5400; or write to Information Services, ASCD, 1703 N. Beauregard St., Alexandria, VA 22311-1714 USA.